DOROTHY M. NOLAN

Metric Cooking

115 EASY RECIPES

GOODHEART-WILLCOX

The Goodheart-Willcox home economics series

Metric Cooking

Dorothy M. Nolan
Home Economics Instructor
Plainview, New York

The Goodheart-Willcox Company, Inc.
South Holland, Illinois

Introduction

Contents

Metric Cooking will help you learn to cook with metric measures. You will learn how to use metric measures in the kitchen, how to follow a recipe, and how to measure ingredients. You will also learn basic guidelines related to kitchen safety.

The recipes in this book are easy to understand and follow. Each recipe includes a list of necessary equipment and step-by-step directions that are clear and complete. All recipes have been tested to help assure successful results.

Metric Cooking includes recipes that will help you develop basic cooking skills and become familiar with kitchen appliances and equipment. The recipes have been designed to fit into short time periods. They can help you prepare nutritious and economical meals quickly and easily.

The metric system of measurement used in this book is in accordance with the standards set forth by the American National Metric Council and the American Home Economics Association.

Copyright 1980 by
THE GOODHEART-WILLCOX CO., INC.
No part of this book may be reproduced in any form without violating the copyright law. Printed in U.S.A.
Library of Congress Catalog Card Number 79-24696.
International Standard Book Number 0-87006-293-X.
12345-80-543210

Library of Congress Cataloging in Publication Data
Nolan, Dorothy M.
  Metric cooking.
  Includes index.
  1. Cookery.   2. Metric system.   I. Title.
TX715.N784   641.5   79-24696
ISBN 0-87006-293-X

1

Kitchen basics

Stepping into the kitchen for the first time can be an exciting and rewarding experience. But some cooks find it disappointing and frustrating instead. Beginning cooks can avoid disappointments by learning commonly used measurements and basic kitchen procedures before they start to cook. Both beginning and experienced cooks can avoid accidents by reviewing safety guidelines.

METRICS IN THE KITCHEN

The metric system of measurement is not new. It has been used in many parts of the world for a long time. Products such as skis and film have been sold in the United States in metric sizes for many years. Cooks in large institutions, such as school cafeterias, have been cooking with metric recipes for many years. But the metric system has just recently moved into the home kitchen.

In the home kitchen, almost all foods are measured by volume. Liquid, dry and small measures are available in metric sizes. Liquid measures are made of glass or plastic. They have a pouring spout and are used to measure foods such as milk and syrup. Dry measures are made of metal or plastic. They are used to measure foods such as flour and sugar. Small measures are used to measure small amounts of both liquid and dry foods.

Some foods, such as potatoes, meat and coffee, are measured by weight. A few foods, such as butter and margarine, can be measured by weight or volume. One recipe may call for 250 mL butter. Another may call for 225 g butter. (Both of these amounts are equivalent to one conventional cup of butter.)

COMMON MEASURES		
	Metric	**Conventional**
Liquid Measures	250 mL	1 cup
	500 mL	2 cups
	1000 mL	1 quart
Dry Measures	50 mL	1/4 cup
	125 mL	1/2 cup
	250 mL	1 cup
Small Measures	1 mL	1/4 teaspoon
	2 mL	1/2 teaspoon
	5 mL	1 teaspoon
	15 mL	1 tablespoon
	25 mL	1/8 cup

Oven thermostat markings are given in degrees Celsius rather than degrees Fahrenheit. A moderately hot oven, for example, is 190 °C to 200 °C.

OVEN THERMOSTAT MARKINGS			
deg. C	**deg. F**	**deg. C**	**deg. F**
100	200	190	375
120	250	200	400
140	275	220	425
150	300	230	450
160	325	240	475
180	350	260	500

Most cooking utensils are sized according to volume. Saucepans, for example, are available in 1 L, 2 L and 3 L sizes. Most baking utensils are sized according to their dimensions. Round cake pans, for example, may be 20 cm by 4 cm or 23 cm by 4 cm. Skillets and casseroles are exceptions. Skillets (cooking utensils) are measured in centimetres. Casseroles (baking utensils) are measured in litres.

UTENSIL	METRIC MEASURE	CONVENTIONAL MEASURE
Saucepan	1 L	1 quart
	2 L	2 quart
	3 L	3 quart
Skillet	15 cm	6 in.
	25 cm	10 in.
	30 cm	12 in.
Baking or cake pan	20 cm by 20 cm by 5 cm	8 in. by 8 in. by 2 in.
	23 cm by 23 cm by 5 cm	9 in. by 9 in. by 2 in.
	33 cm by 23 cm by 5 cm	13 in. by 9 in. by 2 in.
Cookie sheet	41 cm by 28 cm	16 in. by 11 in.
	46 cm by 30 cm	18 in. by 12 in.
Jelly roll pan	39 cm by 27 cm by 3 cm	15 1/2 in. by 10 1/2 in. by 1 in.
Loaf pan	19 cm by 10 cm by 6 cm	7 1/2 in. by 3 3/4 in. by 2 1/4 in.
	23 cm by 13 cm by 8 cm	9 in. by 5 in. by 3 in.
Round cake pan	20 cm by 4 cm	8 in. by 1 1/2 in.
	23 cm by 4 cm	9 in. by 1 1/2 in.
Pie plate	20 cm by 3 cm	8 in. by 1 1/4 in.
	23 cm by 3 cm	9 in. by 1 1/4 in.
Tube pan	25 cm by 10 cm	10 in. by 4 in.
Casserole	1 L	1 quart
	1.5 L	1 1/2 quart
	2 L	2 quart
	3 L	3 quart
Custard cup	200 mL	6 ounces

Sometimes you may want to convert conventional recipes to the metric system. A conversion chart can help you do so. However, keep in mind that no two systems of measurement are exactly alike. Recipes that are converted from one system of measurement to another should be tested. (All recipes in this book have been tested.)

BASIC KITCHEN PROCEDURES

Organization is as important in the kitchen as it is in a science laboratory. Following a logical sequence of steps will help you obtain a successful product.

The first step is to read the recipe carefully from start to finish. This tells you what ingredients and equipment you will need, what pre-preparation steps

CONVERSION FACTORS

LENGTH			LIQUID MEASURE		
	Multiply by			**Multiply by**	
millimetres to inches		0.039	millilitres to ounces		0.034
centimetres to inches		0.394	litres to pints		2.1
inches to millimetres		25.40	litres to quarts		1.056
inches to centimetres		2.540	litres to gallons		0.264
			ounces to millilitres		29.573
WEIGHT			pints to litres		0.473
	Multiply by		quarts to litres		0.946
grams to ounces		0.035	gallons to litres		3.785
grams to pounds		0.002			
kilograms to pounds		2.2	ENERGY		
ounces to grams		28.350		**Multiply by**	
pounds to grams		454	kilocalorie to kilojoule		4.184
pounds to kilograms		0.454	kilojoule to kilocalorie		0.239

TEMPERATURE

Fahrenheit to Celsius: degree C = 5/9 x (F — 32)   Celsius to Fahrenheit: degree F = (9/5 x C) + 32

are required, and how long the product must cook or bake.

The next step is to gather all of the ingredients you will need. Then gather all of the equipment you will need. These items can be placed on separate trays to help keep kitchen counters neat and organized.

Measuring ingredients takes a careful eye. When measuring liquid ingredients such as milk, set the measure on a flat surface. Then add the liquid. When you check to see if the right amount of liquid is in the measure, be sure to look at the liquid at eye level. If you look up or down at the liquid, your measurement may not be accurate.

When measuring dry ingredients such as flour, lightly spoon the ingredient into the measure. Use a straight-edged spatula to level the ingredient so it is even with the top edge of the measure. Do not press dry ingredients down into the measure. If you do, you will pack too much into the measure. Brown sugar is an exception to this rule. Most recipes assume that brown sugar will be packed into the dry measure.

Fats can be measured in several different ways. Soft fats, such as hydrogenated vegetable shortening, can be measured by pressing the fat firmly into the measure with a rubber spatula. The top of the fat is smoothed so it is level with the top of the measure. Some fats, such as butter and margarine, are packaged in 125 mL sticks. You can cut just the amount of fat you need from the stick. Hard fats, such as lard, can be measured by water displacement. Subtract the amount of fat you need from 250 mL. Put that amount of water into a liquid measure. Then add enough fat to make the water reach the 250 mL level. (Be sure the fat is covered by the water.) Drain the water, and the right amount of fat is ready for use.

Once all of the ingredients have been measured, complete any pre-preparation steps. These steps include preheating the oven, greasing baking pans, melting chocolate or butter, separating eggs, chopping nuts and grating lemon rind. Then you will be ready to follow the main steps in the recipe to prepare the food product.

SAFETY IN THE KITCHEN

Many accidents occur in the kitchen. Cuts, burns, falls and other common kitchen accidents can be prevented if you are careful. Be sure to follow basic safety guidelines at all times.

Cuts

Most kitchen cuts are caused by broken glass or sharp knives. A few are caused by improper handling of appliances with sharp blades. The following guidelines can help prevent kitchen cuts.

Always wear rubber gloves to pick up large pieces of broken glass. Sweep smaller fragments into a disposable dustpan. Pick up any remaining fragments with a damp paper towel. Dispose of all broken glass away from other people and pets.

Open cans carefully. Many lids have sharp edges. Dispose of can lids by wrapping them securely in paper towels.

Keep knives sharp. A dull knife may slip during use and cause a cut.

Wash knives and other sharp objects separately. If you put them into the dishwater with other dishes, you may cut yourself as you try to pick them up.

Dry knives by wiping along the dull side with a heavy towel. Store knives away from other utensils.

Use knives properly. Do not use them as hammers or screwdrivers.

If a knife should slip off a work surface, let it fall. Do not try to grab it in midair.

Do not place your fingers or utensils near the beaters or blades of mixers, blenders and food processors. If food becomes stuck, disconnect the appliance and use a nonmetallic object to dislodge it.

Burns

Most kitchen burns are caused by electrical appliances, hot cooking and baking utensils, spattering grease and scalding liquids. The following guidelines can help prevent kitchen burns.

Check to see that all electrical appliances have the Underwriters Laboratories seal of approval.

Be sure all electrical appliances are grounded.

Always follow manufacturer's instructions carefully when using any appliance. If an appliance should malfunction, disconnect it immediately and contact an authorized repair person.

Turn the controls of all electrical appliances to the off position when not in use. Disconnect all small appliances.

Never stand on a wet floor when using an electrical appliance. Never use an electrical appliance on a wet or damp counter.

Always use pot holders when handling hot cooking and baking utensils. Be sure the pot holders are dry.

Wet pot holders can cause painful steam burns.

Turn all pan handles away from the front edge of the range to prevent accidental tipping.

Wear tight-fitting clothes when working near the range. If your hair is long, tie it back away from your face.

When frying, carefully watch the pan containing the hot fat. If a fire should start, use salt, baking soda or a fire extinguisher to extinguish the flames. Never use water.

To avoid a steam burn, remove lids from hot pans carefully. Hold the pan at an angle and tip the lid away from yourself.

When lighting a gas range manually, light the match before you turn on the gas.

Falls

Most kitchen falls are caused by spilled food and unsteady step stools. The following guidelines can help prevent many kitchen falls.

If food or liquid is spilled on the floor, wipe it up immediately. Clean the area thoroughly to be sure no greasy residue remains.

When waxing the kitchen floor, apply the wax in a thin layer. Allow the wax to dry thoroughly before walking across the floor.

Avoid loose throw rugs. If a throw rug must be used, be sure it has a nonskid backing.

Do not use a chair or box to reach high cabinet shelves. Use a sturdy ladder or step stool instead.

Other kitchen hazards

Other kitchen hazards include open cabinet doors and drawers, aerosol cans and pressure cookers.

Cabinet doors and drawers should be kept closed. Bumping into an open cabinet door or drawer can cause a painful bruise. If doors have magnetic closures, be sure the closures are kept in good repair.

Products in aerosol cans should be used away from any heat source. They should be stored in a cool place and disposed of properly. Never burn aerosol cans. Even if they seem empty, they may contain enough propellant to explode when heated.

Before using a pressure cooker, read the manufacturer's use and care booklet carefully. Always wait until the pressure in the canner has reached zero before removing the cover.

These simple precautions can save you from minor frustrations as well as from painful injuries. If you follow safety guidelines and basic kitchen procedures, your cooking experiences will be safe, fun and rewarding.

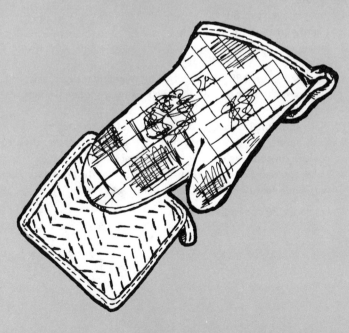

2

Super snacks

CRUNCHY WHEAT GERM BALLS

Ingredients:

250 mL flour	1/2 egg
125 mL wheat germ	2 mL grated orange peel
125 mL margarine, softened	3 mL vanilla
100 mL sugar	50 mL additional wheat germ
1 mL salt	

Equipment:

Small measures, large dry measures, narrow metal spatula, grater, waxed paper, cookie sheet, custard cup, fork, large mixing bowl, wooden spoon, electric mixer (optional), wide spatula, cooling rack.

Procedure:

1. Preheat oven to 180 °C.
2. Lightly grease a cookie sheet.
3. Break egg into a custard cup. Mix with a fork and divide evenly. Share half with another group.
4. Combine flour, 125 mL wheat germ, margarine, sugar, salt, egg, orange peel and vanilla in a large mixing bowl. Mix well using a wooden spoon or electric mixer. Beat 2 minutes.
5. Place additional wheat germ on a sheet of waxed paper.
6. With hands, roll dough into balls, 2.5 cm in diameter, then roll in wheat germ. Place cookies on cookie sheet about 5 cm apart.
7. Bake cookies 12 to 15 minutes or until lightly browned. Remove from cookie sheet with wide spatula and cool on cooling rack.

Makes about 20 cookies.

BRAN REFRIGERATOR COOKIES

Ingredients:

1/2	egg		250	mL light brown sugar, firmly packed
375	mL flour		125	mL whole bran cereal
5	mL baking powder		125	mL walnuts, finely chopped
125	mL margarine, softened			

Equipment:

Small measures, large dry measures, narrow metal spatula, rubber spatula, wooden spoon, cutting board, French knife, waxed paper, custard cup, fork, medium mixing bowl, electric mixer (optional), 2 cookie sheets, wide spatula, cooling racks.

Procedure:

1st Day

1. Break egg into a custard cup. Mix with a fork and divide evenly. Share half with another group.
2. Combine flour and baking powder on a sheet of waxed paper; set aside.
3. Place margarine in medium mixing bowl. Beat with wooden spoon or electric mixer until creamy. Add brown sugar gradually and beat mixture until light and fluffy.
4. Add egg and beat well.
5. Stir in bran cereal, nuts, flour and baking powder. (Mixture will be stiff so use hands if necessary.)
6. On a sheet of waxed paper, shape dough into a long roll, about 4 cm in diameter. Wrap well and refrigerate until ready to use.

2nd Day

1. Preheat oven to 200 °C.
2. Lightly grease 2 cookie sheets.
3. Unwrap cookie dough. With a sharp knife, slice cookies 6 mm thick.
4. Place cookies on cookie sheets 5 cm apart.
5. Bake cookies about 8 minutes, or until lightly browned.
6. Remove from cookie sheet and transfer to cooling racks.

Makes about 3 dozen cookies.

HONEY-NUTTERS

Ingredients:

125 mL peanut butter	8 squares graham crackers
75 mL honey	50 mL instant nonfat dry milk powder
125 mL coconut or wheat germ	

Equipment:

Large dry measures, small liquid and dry measures, narrow metal spatula, rubber spatula, medium mixing bowl, waxed paper, rolling pin, wooden spoon, serving plate.

Procedure:

1. Combine peanut butter and honey in medium mixing bowl.
2. Put coconut or wheat germ on a sheet of waxed paper.
3. Put graham crackers between 2 sheets of waxed paper. Use a rolling pin to crush crackers into fine crumbs.
4. Add nonfat dry milk and graham crackers to peanut butter and honey mixture in mixing bowl. Mix well with wooden spoon.
5. Shape mixture with hands into balls the size of walnuts.
6. Roll balls in coconut or wheat germ, coating each evenly. Place coated cookies on a plate.

Makes 10 to 12 snacks.

CALICO RELISH DIP

Ingredients:

125 mL commercial sour cream	30 mL scallions, minced
50 mL mayonnaise	30 mL radishes, minced
5 mL sugar	30 mL green pepper, minced
2 mL salt	1/2 clove garlic, minced

Equipment:

1 L mixing bowl with cover, small liquid and dry measures, large dry measures, cutting board, French knife, wooden spoon.

Procedure:

1st Day

1. Put sour cream and mayonnaise into mixing bowl.
2. Add sugar and salt to sour cream mixture and stir with wooden spoon.
3. Add vegetables, stirring well with wooden spoon. Cover dip tightly and refrigerate at least 2 hours to allow flavors to blend.

2nd Day

1. Put dip into serving dish.
2. Serve dip with assorted fresh vegetables.

Makes 250 mL dip.

DEVILED EGGS

Ingredients:

4 eggs
  pinch salt
  pinch pepper

1 mL dry mustard
30 mL mayonnaise
  dash paprika

Equipment:

1 L saucepan with cover, small mixing bowl, fork, knife, small liquid and dry measures, serving dish.

Procedure:

1st Day

1. Place the eggs in a 1 L saucepan. Cover with cold water. Heat water to the boiling point. Remove pan from heat and cover immediately. Let eggs stand for 20 minutes.
2. Run eggs under cold water to cool. Refrigerate until ready to use.

2nd Day

1. Shell hard-cooked eggs. (Tap ends to crack shell, then roll between hands to loosen shells; peel.)
2. Cut each egg in half. Remove yolks and place in small mixing bowl. Place whites on a serving dish.
3. Mash egg yolks with a fork. Add salt, pepper, dry mustard and mayonnaise and mix well. (If mixture looks dry, add a little more mayonnaise.)
4. Fill egg white shells with yolk mixture, dividing mixture evenly. Sprinkle with paprika.

Makes 4 appetizer servings or 8 snacks.

QUICK AND EASY PIZZA

Ingredients:

5 biscuits (1/2 can) refrigerated biscuits
125 mL mozzarella cheese, shredded
125 mL spaghetti sauce

  dash oregano
  dash garlic powder (optional)

Equipment:

Large liquid and dry measures, rubber spatula, grater, waxed paper, cookie sheet, cutting board, wide spatula.

Procedure:

1. Preheat oven to 220 °C.
2. Lightly grease a large cookie sheet.
3. Pat each biscuit into a circle about 10 cm across on a cutting board. (Biscuits also may be rolled with a rolling pin.)
4. Transfer biscuits to cookie sheet with wide spatula.
5. Spread about 15 mL of sauce on each biscuit.
6. Sprinkle sauce with cheese, dividing cheese evenly between biscuits.
7. Sprinkle cheese with oregano and garlic powder.
8. Bake pizzas about 10 minutes or until cheese is bubbly and crust is lightly browned.
9. Remove pizzas from cookie sheet with wide spatula and serve immediately.

Makes 5 small pizzas.

SWISS CHEESE DREAMS

Ingredients:

250 mL Swiss cheese (coarsely grated and lightly packed)

10 stuffed olives, chopped

45 mL mayonnaise

2 whole English muffins

Equipment:

Small and large dry measures, grater, French knife, cutting board, rubber spatula, small mixing bowl, cookie sheet, wide spatula.

Procedure:

1. Preheat oven to 190 °C.
2. Combine cheese, olives and mayonnaise in small mixing bowl.
3. Cut English muffins into halves, then in quarters (16 pieces).
4. Spread cheese mixture on muffins (dividing mixture evenly).
5. Place snacks on an ungreased baking sheet. Bake until bubbly, about 10 to 15 minutes.
6. Remove snacks from cookie sheet with wide spatula and serve immediately.

Makes 16 snacks.

TUNA CRESCENTS

Ingredients:

1/2 of 250 g can tuna fish, drained and flaked

15 mL celery, finely chopped

15 mL mayonnaise

dash Worcestershire sauce

5 biscuits (1/2 can) refrigerated biscuits

Equipment:

Cookie sheet, cutting board, French knife, small liquid and dry measures, small mixing bowl, rubber spatula, fork, wide spatula.

Procedure:

1. Preheat oven to 200 °C.
2. Lightly grease a cookie sheet.
3. Place tuna in a small mixing bowl.
4. Add celery, mayonnaise and Worcestershire sauce and mix well.
5. On floured board, pat or roll each biscuit into a 10 cm round. Divide tuna mixture evenly on the biscuits, placing mixture on one half of each round only. Fold unfilled half dough over filled half; seal edges of crescents with a fork. Prick tops with a fork.
6. Bake crescents about 10 minutes or until golden brown.
7. Remove snacks from cookie sheet with a wide spatula and serve immediately.

Makes 10 snacks.

Spectacular salads

SPINACH SALAD

Ingredients:

1	egg		dash	pepper
3	slices bacon		750	mL spinach, cleaned and dried
15	mL vinegar		30	mL Parmesan cheese
25	mL onion, chopped			

Equipment:
Small saucepan with lid, small skillet, paper towels, cutting board, French knife, salad bowl, salad fork and spoon, small liquid and dry measures, large dry measures, rubber spatula, wooden spoon.

Procedure:
1. Place the egg in a small saucepan. Cover with cold water. Heat water to the boiling point. Remove pan from heat and cover immediately. Let egg stand for 20 minutes.
2. Hold egg under cold running water to cool. Refrigerate until ready to use.
3. Cook bacon in small skillet, over medium heat, until crisp; drain well on paper towels. Reserve 30 mL bacon fat in the skillet.
4. Add vinegar, onion and pepper to bacon fat. Heat until dressing reaches a boil.
5. Shell hard-cooked egg. Chop the egg into small pieces and set aside.
6. Tear spinach into bite-sized pieces and place in salad bowl.
7. Crumble bacon and add to spinach. Add cheese and dressing. Toss lightly.
8. Top salad with chopped hard-cooked egg and serve immediately.

Serves 5 to 6 (small servings).

(Note: Egg can be hard-cooked the day before salad is to be prepared and refrigerated. Spinach can be cleaned, dried and placed in plastic bag in the vegetable crisper.)

COLESLAW

Ingredients:

1/2	small head (about 300 g) cabbage	5	mL lemon juice
2	small carrots	1	mL celery seed
15	mL sugar	50	mL mayonnaise
1	mL salt	125	mL pineapple tidbits, drained

Equipment:

Shredder-grater, large mixing bowl, floating edge vegetable peeler, small mixing bowl, two forks, small liquid and dry measures, large dry measures, rubber spatula.

Procedure:

1. Shred cabbage into large mixing bowl.
2. Clean and scrape carrots. Shred into large mixing bowl.
3. Combine sugar, salt, lemon juice, celery seed and mayonnaise in small mixing bowl.
4. Add dressing and pineapple tidbits to shredded vegetables; toss with two forks until well mixed.
5. Chill coleslaw in covered container until ready to serve.

Serves 3 to 4.

CUCUMBER SALAD

Ingredients:

1	medium cucumber	15	mL soy sauce
1	mL salt	15	mL sugar
15	mL red wine vinegar	5	mL oil

Equipment:

Floating edge vegetable peeler, cutting board, French knife, small mixing bowl, custard cup, small liquid and dry measures, rubber spatula.

Procedure:

1. Peel cucumber and cut into very thin slices. Put slices in small mixing bowl and sprinkle with salt; let stand 10 minutes, then drain well.
2. Combine vinegar, soy sauce, sugar and oil in custard cup.
3. Pour sauce over drained cucumber slices. Chill well before serving.

Serves 3 to 4.

ATHENIAN SALAD

Ingredients:

2 radishes, thinly sliced	1 mL salt
1/4 green pepper, finely chopped	1 mL pepper
1/4 cucumber, thinly sliced	1 mL oregano
1 tomato, cut into wedges	15 mL red wine vinegar
1 stalk celery, diced	30 mL olive oil
3 Greek olives	2.5 cm cube feta cheese, crumbled
1 green onion, sliced	

Equipment:

Cutting board, French knife, salad bowl, glass jar with tightly-fitting cover, salad fork and spoon, small measures.

Procedure:

1. Wash and prepare vegetables as directed.
2. Put radishes, green pepper, cucumber, tomato, celery, olives and onions in salad bowl; toss lightly.
3. Put salt, pepper, oregano, red wine vinegar and olive oil in a jar with a tightly-fitting cover; shake well.
4. Pour dressing over salad and toss lightly. Sprinkle cheese on top.

Serves 3 to 4.

WALDORF SALAD

Ingredients:

250 mL diced apple	5 mL sugar
125 mL celery, diced	1 mL lemon juice
50 mL walnuts, chopped	50 mL heavy cream
30 mL mayonnaise	

Equipment:

Cutting board, French knife, mixing bowl, custard cup, rubber spatula, rotary beater, small mixing bowl, small and large liquid and dry measures.

Procedure:

1. Combine apple, celery and walnuts in mixing bowl.
2. Put mayonnaise, sugar and lemon juice into custard cup. Mix well.
3. Whip heavy cream in small, chilled bowl with a rotary beater. Fold whipped cream into mayonnaise with a rubber spatula. Fold apple mixture into dressing.
4. Refrigerate salad in covered bowl until well-chilled.

Serves 3 to 4.

FROSTED FRUIT SALAD

Ingredients:

2	packages, 85 g each, strawberry-flavored gelatin	2	large bananas
500	mL boiling water	1	can, 432 g, crushed pineapple, drained
1	package, 283 g, frozen strawberries	250	mL sour cream

Equipment:

Large mixing bowl, small saucepan, wooden spoon, small mixing bowl, fork, rubber spatula, large liquid and dry measures, 20 cm square cake pan.

Procedure:

1. In large bowl, combine gelatin and boiling water; stir to dissolve gelatin.
2. Add strawberries, stirring until strawberries are thawed and gelatin begins to thicken.
3. In small bowl, mash bananas with fork.
4. Add drained pineapple to mashed bananas.
5. Fold bananas and pineapple into slightly thickened gelatin.
6. Pour mixture into a 20 cm square cake pan. Refrigerate until set.
7. Frost salad with sour cream. Cut into squares and serve.

Serves 6 to 8.

POTATO SALAD

Ingredients:

6	medium-sized potatoes	2	mL salt
	dash salt	1	mL pepper
2	eggs	175	mL mayonnaise
15	mL onion, chopped		salad greens
50	mL celery, chopped		

Equipment:

Large saucepan, covered container, medium saucepan with lid, cutting board, French knife, large mixing bowl, rubber spatula, small measures, large dry measures, salad bowl.

Procedure:

1st Day

1. Wash, peel and halve potatoes.
2. Put potatoes in large saucepan. Cover with slightly salted water. Simmer until tender (about 25 to 30 minutes). Drain and refrigerate in covered container.
3. Place eggs in medium saucepan. Cover with cold water. Heat water to the boiling point. Remove pan from heat and cover immediately. Let eggs stand for 20 minutes.
4. Hold eggs under cold running water to cool. Refrigerate.

2nd Day

1. Slice or cube potatoes and put in large mixing bowl.
2. Add onion and celery to potatoes. Mix.
3. Add salt, pepper and mayonnaise; mix well with rubber spatula.
4. Shell hard-cooked eggs. Cut into wedges.
5. Serve potato salad in a bowl lined with salad greens. Garnish with hard-cooked egg wedges.

Serves 3 to 4.

MACARONI SALAD

Ingredients:

500	mL cooked macaroni	dash pepper
30	mL celery, chopped	175 mL mayonnaise
15	mL onion, chopped	salad greens
15	mL green pepper, chopped	parsley
1	tomato	paprika
2	mL salt	

Equipment:

Large saucepan, covered container, large mixing bowl, cutting board, French knife, rubber spatula, large dry measures, small measures.

Procedure:

1st Day

1. Cook macaroni according to package directions. (Use 250 mL uncooked macaroni.)
2. Drain macaroni and refrigerate in a covered container.

2nd Day

1. Put cooked macaroni in a large bowl.
2. Add celery, onion and green pepper.
3. Cut tomato into bite-sized pieces and add to macaroni. Using rubber spatula, fold in salt, pepper and mayonnaise.
4. Serve salad in a bowl lined with salad greens. Garnish with parsley and paprika.

Serves 3 to 4.

GREAT CHICKEN SALAD

Ingredients:

500	mL chicken, cubed	125 mL celery, diced
	(Chicken can be either	2 mL salt
	canned or stewed, cooled	dash pepper
	and drained.)	50 to 75 mL mayonnaise
125	mL pineapple tidbits, drained	Salad greens or
125	mL Swiss cheese, diced	pineapple shell

Equipment:

Cutting board, French knife, large mixing bowl, rubber spatula, small measures, large dry measures.

Procedure:

1. Combine chicken, pineapple, Swiss cheese and celery in large mixing bowl.
2. Add salt, pepper and 50 mL mayonnaise to chicken mixture. Stir with rubber spatula until moistened. (If salad seems dry, add 25 mL more mayonnaise.)
3. Chill salad until ready to serve. Serve on a bed of salad greens or in a pineapple shell.

Serves 3 to 4.

CHEF'S SALAD

Ingredients:

1/2 head iceberg lettuce	125 mL Swiss cheese
1/4 bunch romaine or endive	dressing
50 mL green onion, chopped	croutons (optional)
50 mL celery, sliced	
125 mL cold, cooked meat (beef, ham or chicken)	

Equipment:

Salad bowl, cutting board, French knife, jelly roll pan (for croutons), narrow metal spatula (for croutons), large dry measures.

Procedure:

1. Clean iceberg lettuce and romaine or endive; drain well and pat dry. Break greens into bite-sized pieces and put in salad bowl.
2. Add onion and celery to greens.
3. Cut meat and cheese into julienne (match-like) strips. Add to greens.
4. Serve salad with your favorite dressing. Sprinkle with croutons if desired.

Serves 3 to 4.

Easy Croutons

1. Cut buttered bread into cubes. Toast in oven. Butter may be seasoned with oregano, basil, or other herbs.

BASIC OIL AND VINEGAR DRESSING

Ingredients:

50 mL salad oil	2 mL salt
30 mL vinegar	1 mL pepper

Equipment:

Small liquid and dry measures, 250 mL liquid measure, glass jar with tightly-fitting cover.

Procedure:

1. Put all ingredients into a jar with a tightly-fitting cover. Shake well.
2. Refrigerate dressing until ready to use. Shake again before using.

Makes 80 mL dressing (enough for 3 to 4 servings).

Variations:

French Dressing

Add 1 mL each of dry mustard and paprika to basic recipe.

Garlic Dressing

Add 1 clove of garlic, minced or crushed, to the basic recipe.

Herb Dressing

Add 5 mL chopped parsley and dash of thyme, basil and oregano to the basic recipe.

SOUR CREAM DRESSING

Ingredients:

80 mL salad oil	1/2 clove garlic
30 mL white wine vinegar	5 mL tomato paste
5 mL salt	60 mL sour cream
dash pepper	15 mL parsley, fresh
2 mL mustard	

Equipment:

Small and large liquid and dry measures, electric blender, small bowl, rubber spatula.

Procedure:

1. Put all ingredients except parsley into blender. Blend 10 seconds.
2. Pour dressing into bowl. Add parsley and mix well with rubber spatula. Refrigerate until ready to use.

Makes about 175 mL dressing.

BASIC COOKED SALAD DRESSING

Ingredients:

30 mL flour	175 mL milk
15 mL sugar	1 egg yolk
2 mL salt	30 mL vinegar
2 mL dry mustard	7 mL margarine

Equipment:

Large liquid measure, small measures, fork, wooden spoon, small saucepan, small bowl.

Procedure:

1. Put flour, sugar, salt and dry mustard in saucepan. Stir well with wooden spoon.
2. Combine milk and egg yolk in liquid measure. Mix with fork to blend.
3. Add liquid ingredients to dry ingredients, slowly, stirring constantly with wooden spoon.
4. Cook mixture over moderate heat, stirring constantly, until it thickens and comes to a boil. Cook one minute longer.
5. Remove dressing from heat and stir in vinegar and margarine. Pour into bowl and refrigerate until well-chilled.

Makes 250 mL dressing.

Variations:

Sour Cream Dressing

Add 125 mL sour cream, 10 mL chopped chives and dash of black pepper to 125 mL cooked dressing.

Russian Dressing

Add 50 mL chili sauce, 5 mL lemon juice and a few drops of onion juice to 125 mL cooked dressing.

4

Vegetable extravaganza

FRENCH ONION SOUP

Ingredients:

3 large onions	1 mL salt
30 mL margarine	dash pepper
3 beef bouillon cubes	3 to 4 slices French bread
2 mL Worcestershire sauce	30 mL grated Parmesan cheese

Equipment:
Cutting board, French knife, medium saucepan, large glass liquid measure, small liquid and dry measures, wooden spoon.

Procedure:

1. Remove papery skin from onions. On cutting board, slice onions thinly with French knife.
2. Melt margarine in medium saucepan. Add onions and sauté until tender and slightly brown.
3. Put bouillon cubes in large glass liquid measure. Add 750 mL boiling water.
4. When onions are tender, add bouillon, Worcestershire sauce, salt and pepper; heat thoroughly.

To Serve: Toast French bread under broiler. Place one slice in each soup bowl and cover with hot soup. Sprinkle with cheese and serve.

Serves 3 to 4.

(Note: Soup may be made the day before, refrigerated and reheated. Add bread and cheese just before serving.)

MINESTRONE SOUP

Ingredients:

2	onions	1	package, 283 g, green beans, frozen
3 to 4	stalks celery	1	can, 454 g, tomatoes, canned
3 to 4	carrots	2	cans, 567 g each, cannellini beans,
2 to 3	zucchini		drained
3 to 4	cloves garlic	1	package, 283 g, peas, frozen
1	head, 450 g, cabbage		salt to taste
45	mL salad oil	2	L water
45	mL margarine	10	mL salt
15	mL basil	250	mL thin spaghetti, broken into
15	mL dried parsley		2 cm pieces
2	L water		grated Romano cheese

Equipment:

Cutting board, floating edge vegetable peeler, French knife, large soup kettle, fork, wooden spoon, small and large liquid and dry measures, large saucepan.

Procedure:

1st Day

1. Wash and dry all fresh vegetables. Dice onions, celery, carrots and zucchini. Mince garlic and shred cabbage.
2. Heat oil and margarine in a large kettle. Add onions, garlic, celery, basil and parsley. Sauté until vegetables are soft but not brown.
3. Add water to vegetables and bring to a boil.
4. Add green beans, carrots, zucchini, and tomatoes. Bring soup to a boil; reduce heat and simmer for 10 minutes.
5. Add cabbage and one can of cannellini beans. Mash the remaining beans with a fork and add to soup. Simmer soup 10 minutes longer.
6. Add peas and salt to taste. Simmer soup until vegetables are tender.
7. Cool soup and refrigerate overnight in a covered container. (This will give flavors a chance to blend.)

2nd Day

1. Bring 2 L of water to a boil in a separate saucepan. Add 10 mL salt and the broken spaghetti. Cook spaghetti until tender, 7 to 8 minutes.
2. Meanwhile, heat soup until it reaches serving temperature. Drain spaghetti and add to soup.
3. Serve soup with grated cheese.

Serves 12 to 16.

GREEN BEAN CASSEROLE

Ingredients:

30 mL margarine	dash pepper
125 mL onion, finely chopped	125 mL Swiss cheese, shredded
30 mL flour	500 mL green beans, canned
5 mL granulated chicken bouillon	125 mL french fried onions,
250 mL milk	crumbled
2 mL salt	

Equipment:

Small saucepan, cutting board, French knife, wooden spoon, wire whisk, shredder-grater, waxed paper, 1 L casserole, small and large liquid and dry measures.

Procedure:

1. Preheat oven to 180 °C.
2. In small saucepan, melt margarine. Add onions and saute' until tender, about 5 minutes. Remove from heat.
3. Add flour and chicken bouillon granules to margarine and onions; stir with wire whisk until smooth.
4. Gradually add milk to flour-margarine mixture, stirring until smooth.
5. Cook sauce over moderate heat, stirring constantly until thickened.
6. Remove sauce from heat. Add salt, pepper and cheese, stirring gently until cheese melts.
7. Add green beans to sauce and pour into greased casserole.
8. Sprinkle casserole with onions.
9. Bake casserole uncovered until bubbly, about 20 minutes.

Serves 3 to 4.

GLAZED CARROTS

Ingredients:

4 medium carrots	30 mL margarine
salt	50 mL brown sugar, firmly packed

Equipment:

Floating edge vegetable peeler, French knife, cutting board, small saucepan with lid, medium saucepan, small liquid and dry measures, wooden spoon.

Procedure:

1. Wash and scrape carrots. Cut crosswise into 2.5 cm chunks.
2. Bring 125 mL lightly salted water to a boil in small saucepan. Add carrots, cover, and cook until crisp-tender (about 15 minutes); drain carrots well.
3. Melt margarine and sugar together in medium saucepan. Add drained carrots. Cook over low heat, turning occasionally, until carrots are well-glazed, about 5 minutes.

Serves 3 to 4.

BROCCOLI WITH CHEESE SAUCE

Ingredients:

1	package, 284 g, broccoli, frozen chopped	250	mL milk
30	mL margarine	125	mL American cheese, shredded
30	mL flour		salt and pepper

Equipment:

Medium saucepan, small saucepan, 1 L casserole, shredder-grater, waxed paper, wire whisk (or wooden spoon), small and large liquid and dry measures, rubber spatula.

Procedure:

1. Preheat oven to 180 °C.
2. Cook broccoli, according to package directions, just until crisp-tender. (Do not overcook.) Drain well and transfer to greased casserole.
3. Put margarine in small saucepan and melt over low heat. Remove from heat.
4. Add flour and stir with wire whisk until smooth. Add milk slowly, stirring with wire whisk until smooth.
5. Return sauce to heat. Cook over moderate heat, stirring constantly, until thickened.
6. Remove sauce from heat. Add cheese and salt and pepper to taste. Stir gently until cheese melts.
7. Pour sauce over broccoli.
8. Bake casserole uncovered until bubbly, about 20 minutes.

Serves 3 to 4.

CORN SESAME SAUTÉ

Ingredients:

500	mL corn, canned	30	mL chopped green pepper
50	mL margarine	2	mL salt
30	mL sesame seeds	1	mL pepper
1/2	clove garlic, crushed	1	mL basil

Equipment:

Medium saucepan, small skillet, wooden spoon, small liquid and dry measures, large dry measures, cutting board, French knife.

Procedure:

1. Put corn in medium saucepan. Heat slowly until steaming.
2. Meanwhile, melt margarine in small skillet. Add sesame seeds and saute' until lightly browned. (Stir occasionally with wooden spoon.)
3. Add garlic and green pepper to sesame seeds. Saute', stirring constantly, for 3 more minutes.
4. Drain corn. Add sautéed vegetable mixture, salt, pepper and basil.

Serves 4 to 6.

RATATOUILLE

Ingredients:

```
500   mL sliced fresh vegetables*
 30   mL margarine
      pinch salt and pepper
```

*Choose several of the following vegetables: Green peppers, zucchini, eggplant, tomatoes, mushrooms, broccoli, cauliflower.

Equipment:

Cutting board, French knife, paring knife, large dry measures, small dry and liquid measures, small skillet, wooden spoon, slotted spoon.

Procedure:

1. Clean vegetables and cut into bite-sized pieces.
2. Melt margarine in skillet.
3. Add vegetables to skillet (except tomatoes and green peppers). Sauté until crisp-tender, about 5 minutes.
4. Add tomatoes and green peppers. Cook an additional 5 minutes.
5. Using a slotted spoon, transfer vegetables to a serving dish. Sprinkle with salt and pepper.

Serves 3.

BAKED ONION CASSEROLE

Ingredients:

```
  5   mL salt                      15   mL pimiento, chopped
500   g small white onions, peeled 50   mL cheddar cheese, grated
  1   package, 283 g, peas, frozen 50   mL soft white bread crumbs
  1   can, 298 g, cream of mushroom soup
```

Equipment:

1 L casserole, medium saucepan, large shallow dish, cutting board, French knife, grater, waxed paper, small liquid and dry measures, large dry measures, rubber spatula.

Procedure:

1. Preheat oven to 180 °C.
2. Lightly grease a 1 L casserole.
3. Put salt and enough water to cover onions in a medium saucepan. Add peeled onions; cook uncovered about 20 minutes or until tender. Drain onions well and put in casserole dish. (Reserve 50 mL of cooking liquid.)
4. Put frozen peas in a large shallow dish. Add hot water and let stand until thawed. Drain. Sprinkle thawed peas over onions in casserole.
5. Mix mushroom soup with 50 mL reserved cooking liquid. Add pimiento. Toss vegetables with sauce until well coated.
6. Combine grated cheese and bread crumbs. Sprinkle over vegetables.
7. Bake casserole, uncovered, until hot and bubbly, about 20 minutes.

Serves 6.

BAKED EGGPLANT PARMESAN

Ingredients:

1 medium eggplant	2 mL sugar
dash salt	1 mL paprika
1 clove garlic	dash pepper
15 mL salad oil	dash basil
15 mL flour	250 mL stewed tomatoes, canned
2 mL salt	25 mL grated Parmesan cheese

Equipment:

1 L casserole, paring knife, cutting board, French knife, medium saucepan with lid, small saucepan, small mixing bowl, small liquid and dry measures, large dry measures, wooden spoon.

Procedure:

1. Preheat oven to 190 °C.
2. Lightly grease a 1 L casserole.
3. Wash and peel eggplant; cut into 2.5 cm cubes. In a medium saucepan, cook eggplant, covered, in a small amount of lightly salted water, for 8 minutes; drain well.
4. Peel and mince garlic. Heat oil in small saucepan; add garlic and saute until golden.
5. Combine flour, salt, sugar, paprika, pepper and basil in small mixing bowl; add stewed tomatoes. Add tomato mixture to garlic in saucepan. Cook sauce over medium heat until it boils and thickens slightly.
6. Layer eggplant cubes and tomato mixture in prepared casserole. Top with grated cheese.
7. Bake casserole until bubbly and lightly browned, about 20 minutes.

Serves 6.

HARVARD BEETS

Ingredients:

1 can, 453 g, beets, sliced	30 mL white vinegar
15 mL sugar	75 mL water
15 mL cornstarch	30 mL margarine
dash salt	

Equipment:

Strainer, small bowl (optional), small saucepan, wooden spoon, small liquid and dry measures, large liquid measure.

Procedure:

1. Drain beets in a strainer and set aside. (Note: Beet liquid may be saved in a small bowl and substituted for all or part of the water.)
2. Combine sugar, cornstarch and salt in a small saucepan. Add vinegar and water, stirring until smooth. Bring mixture to a boil, stirring constantly. Simmer sauce until thickened, about 5 minutes.
3. Add sliced beets and margarine. Simmer until beets are hot.

Serves 3.

SKILLET ZUCCHINI

Ingredients:

2 to 3 small zucchini	1 mL salt
1 egg	dash pepper
30 mL flour	30 mL salad oil

Equipment:

Cutting board, French knife, large custard cup, fork, waxed paper, small skillet, small liquid and dry measures.

Procedure:

1. Wash and dry zucchini; slice thinly.
2. Break egg into a large custard cup and beat with a fork.
3. Combine flour, salt and pepper on a sheet of waxed paper.
4. Heat oil in small skillet until hot but not smoking.
5. Dip zucchini slices in egg, then in seasoned flour. Saute slices in oil until tender, about 4 to 5 minutes.

Serves 3 to 4.

ORANGE BUTTER SWEET POTATOES

Ingredients:

4 medium sweet potatoes (or yams)	30 mL orange juice
30 mL margarine	dash salt
5 mL grated orange peel	15 mL sugar

Equipment:

1 L casserole, cutting board, French knife, large saucepan with lid, small saucepan, floating edge vegetable peeler, electric mixer, rubber spatula, small liquid and dry measures.

Procedure:

1. Preheat oven to 190 °C.
2. Lightly grease a 1 L casserole.
3. Wash potatoes and cut into quarters. Place in a large saucepan and add boiling water to cover.
4. Cook potatoes, covered, 15 to 20 minutes or until tender.
5. Combine margarine, orange peel, orange juice, salt and sugar in small saucepan. Simmer uncovered 5 minutes.
6. When potatoes are cooked, drain and peel. Mash with an electric mixer until smooth. Add orange juice mixture, mixing well.
7. Turn potato mixture into casserole. Bake covered for 25 minutes.

Serves 4.

SCALLOPED POTATOES

Ingredients:

3 to 4 medium potatoes (all-purpose)
1 medium onion
dash salt
25 mL flour
1 mL salt

dash pepper
30 mL margarine
250 mL milk
dash paprika

Equipment:

1 L casserole, floating edge vegetable peeler, cutting board, French knife, medium saucepan with lid, custard cup, small saucepan, wire whisk (or wooden spoon), rubber spatula, small liquid and dry measures, large liquid measure.

Procedure:

1. Preheat oven to 200 °C.
2. Lightly grease a 1 L casserole.
3. Wash, pare and thinly slice potatoes.
4. Remove papery skin from onion. Peel and slice thinly.
5. Cook potatoes and onion, in small amount of salted water, in a covered saucepan, until barely tender, about 5 minutes; drain well.
6. Combine flour, salt and pepper in a custard cup.
7. Melt margarine in small saucepan.
8. Add flour mixture to melted margarine, stirring until smooth.
9. Add milk gradually, stirring constantly, until mixture is smooth. Cook sauce over medium heat, stirring constantly, until thickened.
10. In prepared casserole, layer half of the potatoes and onions with half of the sauce. Repeat layers. Sprinkle with paprika.
11. Bake casserole, uncovered, until top is browned and potatoes are tender when pierced with a fork, about 35 minutes.

Serves 3 to 4.

5

Main events

LASAGNE

Ingredients:

15 mL salad oil	5 mL salt
250 g ground beef	2 mL pepper
2 cloves garlic, minced	2 mL oregano
50 mL onion, chopped	225 g package lasagne (pasta)
250 mL tomato paste	250 mL mozzarella cheese, shredded
500 mL tomatoes, canned	250 mL ricotta cheese (or cottage cheese)

Equipment:

Cutting board, French knife, medium skillet (or electric skillet), small and large liquid and dry measures, rubber spatula, large saucepan, 19 by 25 by 4 cm oblong baking dish, shredder-grater, waxed paper.

Procedure:

1st Day

1. Heat oil in medium skillet or electric skillet. Add ground beef and cook until browned; drain excess fat.
2. Add garlic and onion to beef mixture. Cook 2 minutes.
3. Add tomato paste, tomatoes, salt, pepper and oregano to browned meat and bring to a boil. Reduce heat to low and simmer 15 minutes.
4. Cook pasta according to package directions.
5. Lightly grease a 19 by 25 by 4 cm oblong baking dish.
6. Alternate layers of cooked pasta, cheese and sauce until all ingredients have been used.
7. Cover and refrigerate lasagne until ready to bake.

2nd Day

1. Preheat oven to 180 °C.
2. Bake lasagne until bubbly, about 20 to 30 minutes.

Serves 4 to 6.

SPANISH RICE

Ingredients:

250 mL raw white rice	500 mL tomatoes, canned
3 slices bacon, diced	5 mL salt
50 mL onion, finely chopped	1 mL pepper
50 mL green pepper, finely chopped	

Equipment:

Medium saucepan, medium skillet, paper towels, cutting board, French knife, small and large dry measures, 2 L casserole, rubber spatula, wooden spoon.

Procedure:

1st Day

1. Prepare rice according to package directions.
2. In medium skillet, fry bacon until crisp. Remove from skillet and drain on a paper towel.
3. Add onion and green pepper to bacon fat and cook over medium heat until tender.
4. Add bacon, cooked rice, tomatoes, salt and pepper to skillet. Mix well.
5. Pour mixture into a greased 2 L casserole. Cover and refrigerate until ready to use.

2nd Day

1. Preheat oven to 180 °C.
2. Bake casserole, uncovered, until hot, about 20 to 30 minutes. Serve at once.

Serves 4 to 6.

EASY ITALIAN SPAGHETTI

Ingredients:

15 mL salad oil	5 mL salt
500 g ground beef	2 mL pepper
2 cloves garlic, minced	2 mL oregano
175 mL tomato paste	1 225 g package spaghetti
500 mL canned tomatoes	Parmesan cheese, grated

Equipment:

Large skillet with lid, cutting board, French knife, large dry measures, small liquid and dry measures, wooden spoon, covered container, large saucepan.

Procedure:

1st Day

1. Heat oil in large skillet. Add ground beef and garlic. Cook until beef loses its pink color. Drain fat which accumulates.
2. Add tomato paste, tomatoes, salt, pepper and oregano to beef mixture.
3. Cover and simmer sauce 20 minutes.
4. Refrigerate in covered container until ready to use.

2nd Day

1. Cook spaghetti according to package directions. Drain well.
2. Reheat sauce while spaghetti is cooking.
3. Divide spaghetti evenly onto dinner plates. Cover with meat sauce. Sprinkle with Parmesan cheese if desired.

Serves 4 to 6.

SPINACH PIE

Ingredients:

15	mL salad oil	2	mL salt
125	mL green onion, thinly sliced	375	mL milk
2	mL dried dill weed	250	mL cottage cheese, cream style
1	package, 283 g, frozen chopped spinach, thawed	125	mL feta cheese, crumbled
2	eggs	2	mL baking powder
50	mL margarine	2	sheets phyllo
50	mL flour	30	mL margarine, melted

Equipment:

Cutting board, French knife, medium skillet, custard cup, small mixing bowl, fork, large saucepan, small and large liquid and dry measures, rubber spatula, wooden spoon, 20 cm square baking pan, pastry brush.

Procedure:

1st Day

1. Heat oil in medium skillet. Add onion and dill and saute' until tender.
2. Squeeze excess water from spinach and add to skillet. Cook until hot; keep warm.
3. Break eggs, one at a time, into a custard cup. Then place in a small mixing bowl. Beat with a fork.
4. In large saucepan, melt 50 mL margarine. Blend in flour and salt, stirring with a wooden spoon until smooth. Add milk gradually, stirring until smooth. Cook sauce, stirring constantly, until thickened.
5. Add about 125 mL of the cream sauce to the beaten eggs and mix well. Add the warmed eggs to the saucepan and cook several minutes more.
6. Stir in cheeses, spinach mixture and baking powder; set aside.
7. Brush half of 1 sheet of phyllo with the remaining melted margarine. Fold in half to form a 20 by 20 cm square. Place phyllo in greased 20 cm square baking pan. Pour in spinach mixture.
8. Brush second sheet of phyllo with margarine, fold in half and place on top of spinach mixture; tuck in the edges.
9. Cover and refrigerate pie until ready to bake.

2nd Day

1. Remove pie from refrigerator.
2. Preheat oven to 160 °C.
3. Bake pie until lightly browned, about 35 to 40 minutes. Let stand 10 minutes before serving.

Serves 8.

SUPER TUNA NOODLE BAKE

Ingredients:

500 mL cooked noodles	125 mL milk
30 mL margarine	125 mL chopped tomatoes, canned
125 mL onion, chopped	250 mL peas, canned or cooked
1 can, 298 g, cream of mushroom soup	1 can, 250 g, tuna

Equipment:

Cutting board, French knife, 2 L casserole, large saucepan, small saucepan, large mixing bowl, large and small liquid and dry measures, rubber spatula.

Procedure:

1st Day

1. Grease a 2 L casserole.
2. Cook noodles according to package directions. Drain and set aside.
3. Melt margarine in small saucepan. Add onion and cook over low heat until tender.
4. Combine noodles, soup, milk, tomatoes, peas and tuna in large mixing bowl. Mix together with rubber spatula. Add cooked onion.
5. Pour mixture into casserole. Cover and refrigerate until ready to use.

2nd Day

1. Preheat oven to 200 °C.
2. Bake casserole, uncovered, until bubbly, about 20 minutes.

Serves 3 to 4.

CHILI CON CARNE

Ingredients:

30 mL salad oil	750 mL tomatoes, canned
50 mL onion, chopped	15 mL chili powder
50 mL green pepper, chopped	5 mL salt
500 g ground beef	500 mL red kidney beans, drained

Equipment:

Cutting board, French knife, small liquid and dry measures, large dry measures, large skillet with lid, wooden spoon, slotted spoon, small mixing bowl.

Procedure:

1. Heat oil in large skillet. Add onion and green pepper. Saute' until tender. Use a slotted spoon to transfer vegetables to small mixing bowl.
2. Add ground beef to skillet and cook until lightly browned, stirring frequently. (Drain fat as it accumulates.)
3. Add onion, green pepper, tomatoes, chili powder and salt to meat in skillet. Bring mixture to a boil; turn heat to low, cover and simmer for 20 minutes.
4. Add beans and simmer for another 10 minutes. (Add water if chili becomes too thick.)
5. Refrigerate until ready to use.

Serves 6 to 8.

(Note: If possible, chili should be made a day ahead to allow flavors to blend.)

PEPPERY PEDRO

Ingredients:

15	mL shortening	2	mL chili powder
50	mL onion, chopped	2	mL salt
50	mL green pepper, chopped	250	mL tomato sauce
250	g ground beef	2	toasted hamburger buns, halved

Equipment:

Cutting board, French knife, large skillet, medium bowl, small and large liquid and dry measures, wooden spoon, large spoon.

Procedure:

1. Melt shortening in large skillet over medium heat. Add onions and saute' for 1 minute.
2. Add green pepper to skillet and saute' 2 minutes. Set vegetables aside in a bowl.
3. In same skillet, brown ground beef, pouring off fat as it accumulates.
4. Add sauteéd vegetables, chili powder, salt and tomato sauce to ground beef.
5. Simmer mixture, stirring occasionally, until bubbly.
6. Toast buns under broiler. (Watch carefully.)
7. Spoon beef mixture over toasted buns and serve at once.

Serves 4.

QUICHE LORRAINE

Ingredients:

	pastry for a 20 cm pie	1	mL sugar
6	slices bacon		dash cayenne (red pepper)
3	eggs	250	mL Swiss cheese, shredded
375	mL milk or light cream	50	mL onion, minced
2	mL salt		

Equipment:

20 cm pie plate, shredder-grater, waxed paper, French knife, cutting board, small and large liquid and dry measures, medium skillet, paper towels, medium mixing bowl, wide metal spatula, rubber spatula, table knife, fork or wire whisk.

Procedure:

1. Preheat oven to 225 °C.
2. Prepare pastry for a single crust pie according to the instructions given in the Standard Pastry recipe on page 71. Set pie shell aside.
3. Fry bacon in medium skillet until crisp. Drain on paper towels. When cool, break into small bits and sprinkle over the bottom of the pie shell.
4. Break eggs into medium mixing bowl. Beat slightly with fork or wire whisk.
5. Combine milk (or cream), salt, sugar and cayenne. Add to eggs and mix well.
6. Add cheese and onion to custard mixture and pour over bacon bits in pie shell.
7. Bake quiche 15 minutes at 225 °C. Reduce oven temperature to 150 °C and bake 30 minutes more or until knife inserted 2.5 cm from the edge comes out clean.

Serves 4 to 6.

(Note: Quiche may be prepared the day before and reheated, if necessary.)

STUFFED CABBAGE ROLLS

Ingredients:

2	L boiling water	1	egg
1	medium head cabbage	45	mL dry bread crumbs
500	g lean ground beef	250	mL onion, chopped
5	mL salt	250	mL chili sauce
1	mL pepper	50	mL grape jelly
2	mL celery salt	30	mL water
45	mL catsup		

Equipment:

20 cm square baking pan, large saucepan, French knife, cutting board, large mixing bowl, small and large liquid and dry measures, rubber spatula, small saucepan, aluminum foil, pastry brush.

Procedure:

1. Preheat oven to 190 °C.
2. Lightly grease a 20 cm square baking pan.
3. Heat water in large saucepan to a boil; reduce heat to low.
4. Clean cabbage under cool, running water. Cut out and discard hard center core. Place cabbage in the saucepan of hot water; let stand until leaves are flexible and can be removed easily from the head (about 5 minutes). (If necessary, return cabbage to hot water to soften inner leaves.) Separate leaves from head carefully and set aside.
5. In a large bowl, combine ground beef, salt, pepper, celery salt, catsup, egg and bread crumbs. Mix with your hands until mixture is well combined.
6. Using a 50 mL measure, scoop up the meat mixture. With hands, form each scoop into a roll, 5 cm long and 2.5 cm wide.
7. Place each meat roll on a drained cabbage leaf; fold top of leaf toward the center, then fold sides toward center and roll up into an oblong shape.
8. Spread onion evenly over bottom of the baking pan.
9. Arrange cabbage rolls in neat rows on top of onion.
10. In a small saucepan, combine chili sauce, grape jelly and water. Cook over medium heat, stirring until jelly has melted. Pour sauce over cabbage rolls.
11. Cover baking pan tightly with foil, and bake cabbage rolls 1 hour. Remove foi! and brush rolls with sauce; bake uncovered 25 minutes longer.

Serves 4 to 6.

(Note: Cabbage rolls may be prepared ahead up through step 7 and refrigerated.)

INDIVIDUAL MEAT LOAVES

Ingredients:

250	g ground beef	5	mL green pepper, minced
75	mL bread crumbs	1	mL salt
1	egg	1	mL dry mustard
15	mL onion, minced	15	mL tomato sauce

Equipment:

Medium mixing bowl, large dry measures, small liquid and dry measures, wooden spoon, muffin pan, cutting board, French knife.

Procedure:

1. Preheat oven to 190 °C.
2. Grease six muffin cups.
3. Place ground beef in mixing bowl. Add remaining ingredients and mix well with wooden spoon.
4. Divide meat mixture evenly between muffin cups.
5. Bake meat loaves on top rack of oven for 20 to 25 minutes.
6. Remove meat loaves from pans immediately and serve.

Serves 6.

MEATLESS MEATBALLS

Ingredients:

1	hard-cooked egg, finely chopped	2	mL salt
75	mL onion, minced		dash pepper
125	mL celery, finely chopped	30	mL margarine, melted
50	mL walnuts, finely chopped	1	beaten egg
50	mL bread crumbs	10	mL oil
50	mL Swiss cheese, grated	250	mL tomato sauce
1	mL garlic powder		spaghetti or rice

Equipment:

Cutting board, French knife, grater, waxed paper, small and large liquid and dry measures, wide metal spatula, rubber spatula, medium mixing bowl, custard cup, fork, medium skillet, jelly roll pan, medium saucepan, small saucepan with lid.

Procedure:

1. To hard-cook an egg, place the egg in a small saucepan. Cover with cold water. Heat water to the boiling point. Remove pan from heat and cover immediately. Let egg stand for 20 minutes.
2. Hold egg under cold running water to cool. Shell the egg and chop into small pieces.
3. Combine hard-cooked egg, onion, celery and walnuts in medium mixing bowl.
4. Add bread crumbs, grated cheese, garlic powder, salt, pepper and melted margarine. Mix well.
5. Break egg into custard cup. Beat with a fork and add to vegetable mixture. Mix well with hands. Shape into balls the size of walnuts.
6. Heat oil in medium skillet. Add meatballs, a few at a time. Cook over medium heat until lightly browned. Transfer browned meatballs to a jelly roll pan.
7. Heat tomato sauce in medium saucepan. Add browned meatballs and heat through.
8. Prepare spaghetti or rice according to package directions. Serve meatballs over the spaghetti or rice.

Makes 8 to 10 meatballs.

TACOS

Ingredients:

Tortillas
125 mL cornmeal
250 mL flour
1 mL salt
375 mL cold water
1 egg
   salad oil
   hydrogenated vegetable
     shortening

Filling
500 g ground beef
125 mL onion, chopped
1 clove garlic, minced
250 mL tomato sauce
175 mL tomato paste
10 mL chili powder
3 mL salt
1 mL oregano
   dash pepper
   shredded cheddar cheese
   shredded lettuce

Equipment:

Cutting board, French knife, rotary beater, heavy griddle or electric skillet, wide spatula, large and small liquid and dry measures, medium mixing bowl, wooden spoon, large skillet with lid, grater-shredder, waxed paper, pastry brush, two forks or tongs, paper towels.

Procedure:

To prepare tortillas:
1. Put cornmeal, flour, salt, water and egg into medium mixing bowl. Beat with a rotary beater until smooth.
2. Heat a heavy griddle or electric skillet. Brush with salad oil.
3. To form each tortilla, pour about 50 mL batter onto hot griddle. Cook tortillas until edges are dry; turn and cook the other side. (Cooked tortillas can be refrigerated for several days or frozen for longer storage.)

To make taco shells:
1. Put enough hydrogenated vegetable shortening in an electric skillet or other large skillet to make the heated shortening 2.5 cm deep.
2. Place tortilla in hot fat and fold in half with 2 forks or tongs. Fry until crisp. Drain well on paper towels.
3. Continue frying tortillas until all taco shells have been shaped.

To prepare filling:
1. Brown ground beef in large skillet.
2. Add onion and garlic to browned meat and cook several minutes longer. Drain fat.
3. Add tomato sauce, tomato paste, chili powder, salt, oregano and pepper to meat mixture. Bring to a boil. Then reduce heat, cover, and simmer about 20 minutes, stirring occasionally.
4. Spoon filling into taco shells. Sprinkle with shredded cheese and lettuce.

Makes 12 tacos.

LAMB CURRY

Ingredients:

30 mL flour	1 medium apple, chopped
5 mL salt	30 mL celery, chopped
1 mL pepper	175 mL chicken broth or bouillon
7 mL curry powder	5 mL lemon juice
500 g lamb shoulder, cut into 2.5 cm cubes	5 mL lemon rind, grated
30 mL margarine	50 mL raisins
50 mL onion, chopped	1 whole clove, minced
	rice

Equipment:

Cutting board, French knife, paper bag, medium skillet with lid, small and large liquid and dry measures, rubber spatula, grater, waxed paper, plate.

Procedure:

1. Combine flour, salt, pepper and curry powder in small paper bag. Coat lamb cubes by shaking a few at a time in flour mixture. Transfer coated cubes to a plate.
2. Melt margarine in medium skillet. Brown lamb cubes on all sides. Drain off excess fat.
3. Add onion, apple and celery to meat cubes.
4. Combine chicken broth, lemon juice, grated lemon rind, raisins and clove and add to meat mixture.
5. Cover and simmer lamb 30 minutes or until tender.
6. Prepare rice according to package directions. Serve lamb curry over rice.

Serves 3.

(Note: Lamb curry may be prepared a day ahead and refrigerated.)

QUICK FISH FRY

Ingredients:

1 egg	1 mL salt
10 mL milk	15 mL Parmesan cheese
125 mL bread crumbs	500 g fish fillets
1 mL oregano	45 mL oil
1 mL basil	

Equipment:

2 pie plates, fork, waxed paper, large skillet, small liquid and dry measures, large dry measure.

Procedure:

1. Break egg into a pie plate; add milk and beat with a fork.
2. Combine bread crumbs, seasonings and cheese in another pie plate.
3. Dip fish fillets in egg, then in crumb mixture. Place coated fillets on waxed paper.
4. Heat oil in large skillet until hot but not smoking. Add fish fillets and fry until golden brown and flesh flakes easily with a fork.
5. Serve immediately.

Serves 4 to 6.

PIZZA

Ingredients:

1	package active dry yeast		30	mL salad oil
	pinch sugar		125	mL tomato sauce
400	mL flour		250	mL mozzarella cheese, shredded
2	mL salt		30	mL Parmesan cheese, grated
150	mL very warm water, (49 to 54 °C)		15	mL salad oil

Equipment:
Large mixing bowl, wooden spoon, small and large liquid and dry measures, electric mixer, bread board, pastry brush, plastic wrap, cookie sheet, rubber spatula, shredder-grater, waxed paper.

Procedure:

1st Day

1. Put yeast, sugar, 250 mL flour and salt into a large mixing bowl. Mix together with wooden spoon.
2. Add warm water and oil and beat 2 minutes on medium speed of electric mixer.
3. Stir in enough flour to make a moderately stiff dough.
4. Turn dough out onto a lightly floured board. Knead until smooth and elastic, about 5 minutes.
5. Place dough in oiled bowl. Brush top with oil. Cover with plastic wrap and let stand for 15 minutes.
6. Refrigerate dough 2 to 24 hours.

2nd Day

1. Preheat oven to 225 °C.
2. Roll or pat dough into a 25 cm circle on a cookie sheet. Make a rim around the edge.
3. Pour tomato sauce evenly over pizza crust.
4. Sprinkle with shredded mozzarella cheese, then with Parmesan cheese.
5. Drizzle with oil.
6. Bake pizza 10 minutes or until crust is brown and cheese is bubbly.

Serves 3 to 4.

SIMPLE ROAST BEEF

Ingredients:
1 kg beef roast

Equipment:
Roasting pan, meat thermometer.

Procedure:

1. Preheat oven to 180 °C.
2. Place roast, fat side up, in open roasting pan. Insert meat thermometer through the thickest part of the roast so point does not touch fat or bone.
3. Roast meat, uncovered, approximately 50 minutes per kilogram for rare; 60 minutes for medium; 75 minutes for well done.
4. Let roast stand 10 minutes before carving.

Serves 4 to 6.

HAM AND SWISS CASSEROLE

Ingredients:

2 to 3	potatoes		125	mL Swiss cheese, shredded
	salt		250	mL ham cubes
30	mL margarine		50	mL green onions,
30	mL flour			peeled and sliced
250	mL milk			

Equipment:

Cutting board, French knife, medium saucepan, 1 L casserole dish, wooden spoon, small and large liquid and dry measures, shredder-grater, waxed paper, rubber spatula, vegetable peeler.

Procedure:

1st Day

1. Wash and peel potatoes; slice thinly. Cook potatoes in a small amount of salted water for 5 minutes in a medium saucepan. Drain. Put potatoes in lightly greased 1 L casserole dish.
2. Melt margarine in a clean medium saucepan. Add flour all at once, stirring with wooden spoon until smooth. Add milk slowly, stirring constantly until mixture is smooth. Cook sauce over medium heat, stirring constantly until thick.
3. Add cheese to sauce and stir until melted.
4. Add ham and green onion to potatoes in casserole dish.
5. Cover meat and vegetables with sauce, mixing lightly. Cover and refrigerate.

2nd Day

1. Preheat oven to 180 °C.
2. Bake casserole uncovered 30 minutes, or until bubbly.

Serves 3 to 4.

PORK CHOPS CREOLE

Ingredients:

30	mL salad oil			dash salt
4	pork chops, 1.5 cm thick			dash pepper
1/2	can vegetable soup		1	medium bay leaf
50	mL water		2	mL Worcestershire sauce

Equipment:

Large skillet with lid, wide metal spatula, small mixing bowl, small liquid and dry measures, rubber spatula.

Procedure:

1. Heat oil in large skillet until hot but not smoking. Brown chops on both sides.
2. Combine vegetable soup, water, seasonings and Worcestershire sauce.
3. When chops are brown, pour off excess fat. Add soup mixture; cover and simmer for 30 minutes.

Serves 4.

OVEN-FRIED CHICKEN PARMESAN

Ingredients:

1	egg, beaten	2	mL paprika
15	mL milk	2	mL salt
50	mL Parmesan cheese		about 1 kg fryer, cut up
125	mL dry bread crumbs	50	mL margarine

Equipment:

19 by 25 cm baking dish, 2 small mixing bowls, small saucepan, small liquid and dry measures, large dry measures.

Procedure:

1. Preheat oven to 180 °C.
2. Grease a 19 by 25 cm baking dish.
3. Combine egg and milk in one bowl and crumbs, cheese and seasonings in another bowl, mixing well.
4. Rinse and dry chicken pieces.
5. Dip chicken pieces in egg mixture, then in crumbs. Place coated pieces in single layer in baking dish.
6. Melt margarine in small saucepan. Pour over chicken.
7. Bake chicken 1 hour, or until juices run clear when a piece is pierced with a fork.

Serves 4 to 6.

MIXED GRILL

Ingredients:

3	lamb chops		salt
3	slices bacon		pepper
3	small pieces calves liver	1	large tomato
3	mL melted margarine	3	medium mushroom caps

Equipment:

Broiler rack, small saucepan, pastry brush, tongs, cutting board, French knife.

Procedure:

1. Wrap bacon slices around lamb chops; place on broiler rack.
2. Brush liver with melted margarine and place on broiler rack with chops.
3. Broil chops and liver 7.5 cm from heat for 5 minutes. Season with salt and pepper and turn with tongs. Broil 5 minutes longer.
4. Slice tomato into 3 pieces. Brush tomato and mushroom caps with melted margarine. Add to meat on broiler pan. Broil 5 minutes longer or until food reaches the desired degree of doneness. Serve immediately.

Serves 3.

CHICKEN CORDON BLEU

Ingredients:

4	small chicken cutlets
2	slices boiled ham
2	slices Swiss cheese
	pinch salt
	pinch pepper
50	mL flour
1	egg
125	mL dry bread crumbs
30	mL margarine
30	mL salad oil

Sauce:

15	mL margarine
15	mL onion, chopped
15	mL cornstarch
15	mL cold water
175	mL chicken broth
	pinch salt
	pinch pepper
15	mL chopped parsley

Equipment:

Boning knife, French knife, cutting board, meat mallet, 3 pie plates or other flat dishes, fork, waxed paper, large skillet with lid, wide spatula, oven-proof serving dish, small saucepan, wooden spoon, custard cup, small and large liquid and dry measures, rubber spatula.

Procedure:

1. Rinse and dry cutlets. With a sharp knife, make a lengthwise slit in each cutlet to make a pocket.
2. Fold one-half slice of ham and one-half slice of cheese together and insert into the pocket of each cutlet. Pound edges of cutlets together with a meat mallet to seal. (Cutlets also may be pounded thinly and rolled around the ham and cheese. Secure with a toothpick.)
3. Combine salt, pepper and flour in a flat dish.
4. Put egg in another flat dish and beat with fork.
5. Put bread crumbs in another flat dish. Dip each cutlet first into the flour, then into the beaten egg and then into the bread crumbs. Place coated cutlets on waxed paper.
6. In a large skillet, heat margarine and oil together. Saute cutlets until golden brown on both sides. Cook covered over low heat until tender (about 10 minutes). Place cutlets in an oven-proof serving dish. Keep warm until sauce is ready.
7. Melt margarine in a small saucepan and saute onions about 1 minute. Remove from the heat.
8. In a custard cup, combine cornstarch with cold water, stirring until smooth. Add to chicken broth. Add broth to saucepan and cook, stirring constantly, until sauce has thickened. Season with salt and pepper to taste.
9. Pour sauce over chicken cutlets. Garnish with parsley.

Serves 4.

Hot from the oven

MUFFINS

Ingredients:

1/2	egg		250	mL flour
125	mL milk		30	mL sugar
30	mL salad oil or		10	mL baking powder
	melted margarine		2	mL salt

Equipment:

Muffin pan, custard cup, small and large liquid and dry measures, narrow metal spatula, large mixing bowl, rubber spatula, small mixing bowl, flour sifter, fork, wooden spoon.

Procedure:

1. Preheat oven to 200 °C.
2. Grease a 6 cup muffin pan.
3. Break egg into a custard cup and mix with a fork. Divide egg evenly and share half with another group.
4. Combine milk and oil (or margarine) in a small mixing bowl. Add egg and mix together with a fork. Set aside.
5. Place flour, sugar, baking powder and salt in sifter. Sift ingredients together into a large mixing bowl.
6. Make a well in the center of flour mixture. Add liquid ingredients. Stir with a wooden spoon just until dry ingredients are moistened. (Batter will be lumpy. *Do not overstir.)*
7. Push spoonfuls of batter into muffin cups, filling each two-thirds full.
8. Bake muffins for 20 minutes, or until golden brown.

Makes 6 muffins.

(*Note:* Any of the following ingredients may be folded into the batter: 125 mL drained blueberries, 125 mL grated raw apple or 60 mL raisins.)

BEST BRAN MUFFINS

Ingredients:

300 mL flour	250 mL all-bran cereal
15 mL baking powder	250 mL milk
2 mL salt	1 egg
75 mL sugar	50 mL salad oil

Equipment:

Muffin pan, custard cup, fork, small and large liquid and dry measures, narrow metal spatula, rubber spatula, 2 mixing bowls (one medium, one large), wooden spoon.

Procedure:

1. Preheat oven to 200 °C.
2. Grease a 12 cup muffin pan.
3. Combine flour, baking powder, salt and sugar in medium mixing bowl. Stir with a wooden spoon.
4. Put bran cereal and milk into a large mixing bowl; stir with a fork to combine. Let mixture stand 2 minutes or until cereal has softened.
5. Break egg into a custard cup and beat with fork. Add beaten egg and oil to cereal mixture and mix well with wooden spoon.
6. Add dry ingredients to cereal mixture, stirring only until dry ingredients are moistened. *Do not overmix.*
7. Drop spoonfuls of batter into 12 muffin cups.
8. Bake muffins about 20 to 25 minutes or until golden brown.

Makes 12 muffins.

PANCAKES

Ingredients:

250 mL flour	250 mL milk
10 mL baking powder	50 mL margarine, melted and cooled
3 mL salt	oil
1 egg	

Equipment:

Griddle, flour sifter, small and large liquid and dry measures, narrow metal spatula, wide metal spatula, fork, wooden spoon, custard cup, medium mixing bowl.

Procedure:

1. Put flour, baking powder and salt into sifter. Sift into medium mixing bowl.
2. Break egg into custard cup; beat with fork.
3. Add egg, milk and melted margarine to dry ingredients. Stir with a wooden spoon just until dry ingredients are moistened. Batter will be lumpy. *Do not overmix.*
4. Grease griddle lightly with oil. Heat griddle until a few droplets of water dance. Pour small amounts of batter onto hot griddle. When bubbles appear and pancakes look dry around the edges, turn them with a wide metal spatula. Cook the other side until browned.
5. Keep pancakes warm in 100 °C oven while cooking remaining pancakes.

Makes 8 to 10, 10 cm pancakes.

BISCUITS

Ingredients:

250 mL flour
  7 mL baking powder
  2 mL salt

 30 mL hydrogenated vegetable
       shortening
100 mL milk

Equipment:

Cookie sheet, flour sifter, small and large liquid and dry measures, narrow metal spatula, rubber spatula, medium mixing bowl, wide metal spatula, cutting board, round biscuit cutter, pastry blender (or 2 knives), fork, rolling pin.

Procedure:

1. Preheat oven to 220 °C.
2. Lightly grease a cookie sheet.
3. Put flour, baking powder and salt into sifter. Sift ingredients together into a medium mixing bowl.
4. Add shortening to dry ingredients. Using two knives or a pastry blender, cut in shortening until particles are the size of small peas.
5. Add milk to flour mixture all at once. Mix with fork until soft dough forms. (Do not overmix.)
6. Using rubber spatula, turn dough out onto a lightly floured board. Knead 10 to 12 times.
7. Roll dough into a circle 1 cm thick. Cut rounds with floured biscuit cutter. Push leftover pieces together and gently roll again. Repeat step using biscuit cutter.
8. Using wide spatula, transfer biscuits to cookie sheet, placing biscuits 1 cm apart.
9. Bake 10 to 12 minutes, or until lightly browned. Serve immediately.

Makes 8 to 10 biscuits.

POPOVERS

Ingredients:

125 mL flour
  1 mL salt

  1 egg
125 mL milk

Equipment:

Muffin pan, small and large liquid and dry measures, custard cup, 2 L mixing bowl, sifter, rotary beater or electric mixer.

Procedure:

1. Preheat oven to 225 °C.
2. Grease a 6 cup muffin pan well.
3. Sift flour and salt together into mixing bowl.
4. Break egg into custard cup. Add egg and milk to dry ingredients and beat with rotary beater or electric mixer just until smooth. *Do not overbeat.*
5. Pour batter into prepared muffin pan, filling each cup about two-thirds full.
6. Bake popovers 20 minutes. Reduce heat to 180 °C and continue baking 15 minutes longer. *(Do not open oven door to peek.)*
7. Serve popovers immediately with butter or margarine and jelly or honey.

Makes 6 popovers.

QUICK COFFEE CAKE

Ingredients:

Cake:

375	mL	flour
15	mL	baking powder
2	mL	salt
125	mL	sugar
1		egg
50	mL	salad oil
175	mL	milk

Topping:

15	mL	flour
5	mL	cinnamon
15	mL	salad oil
50	mL	brown sugar
125	mL	chopped nuts (optional)

Equipment:

20 cm square cake pan, flour sifter, small and large liquid and dry measures, narrow metal spatula, rubber spatula, large mixing bowl, two small mixing bowls, fork, cutting board, French knife.

Procedure:

1. Preheat oven to 190 °C.
2. Grease a 20 cm square cake pan.
3. Put flour, baking powder, salt and sugar into sifter. Sift into large mixing bowl; set aside.
4. Break egg into small mixing bowl.
5. Add milk and oil to egg, mixing with a fork until blended.
6. Add egg mixture to dry ingredients. Stir with rubber spatula just until dry ingredients are moistened. *Do not overstir.*
7. Using a rubber spatula, spread batter evenly in cake pan.
8. Sprinkle topping evenly over batter.
9. Bake 30 to 35 minutes or until toothpick inserted in the center comes out clean.

Topping

Combine flour, cinnamon, oil and brown sugar in small mixing bowl. Add nuts. Mix topping thoroughly with a fork.

Makes one 20 cm coffee cake.

WILLIAM TELL COFFEE CAKE

Ingredients:

Cake:

375	mL flour
10	mL baking powder
1	mL salt
2	mL nutmeg
50	mL margarine
175	mL sugar
1	egg
5	mL vanilla
150	mL milk

Topping:

2	small apples
75	mL sugar
5	mL cinnamon

Equipment:

23 cm square cake pan, flour sifter, waxed paper, small and large liquid and dry measures, narrow metal spatula, rubber spatula, wooden spoon, medium mixing bowl, small mixing bowl, electric mixer (optional), custard cup, cutting board, French knife, paring knife.

Procedure:

Cake

1. Preheat oven to 190 °C.
2. Grease a 23 cm square cake pan.
3. Put flour, baking powder, salt and nutmeg into sifter. Sift ingredients onto a sheet of waxed paper.
4. Put margarine in medium mixing bowl. Beat with wooden spoon or electric mixer until creamy.
5. Add sugar. Cream margarine and sugar together until fluffy.
6. Break egg into custard cup. Add egg and vanilla to creamed mixture, beating until smooth.
7. Add dry ingredients to creamed mixture alternately with milk beginning and ending with dry ingredients. Beat batter smooth after each addition.
8. Pour batter into greased pan, spreading evenly with rubber spatula.
9. Sprinkle topping evenly over batter.
10. Bake cake 35 to 40 minutes or until toothpick inserted in the center comes out clean.

Topping

1. Peel and core apples; chop finely.
2. Combine sugar, cinnamon and apples in small bowl. Mix well.

Makes one 23 cm coffee cake.

BANANA BREAD

Ingredients:

425 mL flour	2 to 3 small bananas
5 mL baking powder	50 mL shortening
2 mL baking soda	175 mL sugar
1 egg	125 mL walnuts, chopped

Equipment:

24 by 13 cm loaf pan, flour sifter, small liquid and dry measures, large dry measures, narrow metal spatula, rubber spatula, fork, waxed paper, wooden spoon, paring knife, French knife, cutting board, small mixing bowl, custard cup, large mixing bowl, wire cooling rack.

Procedure:

1. Preheat oven to 190 °C.
2. Grease one 24 by 13 cm loaf pan.
3. Put flour, baking powder and baking soda into sifter. Sift ingredients onto a sheet of waxed paper.
4. Break egg into custard cup; beat with fork.
5. Slice bananas into a small bowl and mash well with fork. (You should have 250 mL mashed bananas.)
6. Chop walnuts.
7. Put shortening and sugar into large mixing bowl. Cream together until fluffy.
8. Add egg and mashed banana to creamed mixture, beating until smooth.
9. Add dry ingredients and walnuts. Stir mixture with wooden spoon just until dry ingredients are moistened. *Do not overmix.*
10. Pour batter into prepared pan. Bake 40 minutes or until golden brown and crusty. (Crack in top of loaf is characteristic of fruit breads.)
11. Turn bread out onto cooling rack to cool thoroughly.

Makes one 24 by 13 cm loaf.

IRISH SODA BREAD

Ingredients:

875	mL flour	15	mL caraway seeds
150	mL sugar	125	mL seedless raisins (optional)
5	mL salt	2	eggs, beaten
15	mL baking powder	375	mL buttermilk
5	mL baking soda	30	mL butter, melted

Equipment:

24 by 13 cm loaf pan, flour sifter, large mixing bowl, small and large liquid and dry measures, custard cup, medium mixing bowl, fork, narrow metal spatula, rubber spatula, wooden spoon, cooling rack.

Procedure:

1. Preheat oven to 190 °C.
2. Grease a 24 cm by 13 cm loaf pan.
3. Put flour, sugar, salt, baking powder and baking soda into sifter. Sift ingredients together into large mixing bowl.
4. Add caraway seeds and raisins to dry ingredients.
5. Break eggs into a custard cup one at a time. Put in medium mixing bowl and beat with a fork until blended.
6. Add buttermilk and melted butter to beaten eggs. Mix well.
7. Add liquid ingredients to dry ingredients. Mix with a wooden spoon just until dry ingredients are moistened. *Do not overmix.*
8. Pour batter into greased pan. Bake 1 hour or until golden brown.
9. Turn bread out onto cooling rack to cool thoroughly.

Makes one 24 by 13 cm loaf.

EASY WHITE BREAD

Ingredients:

625 to 750 mL flour
  15 mL sugar
   7 mL salt
   1 package active dry yeast

  30 mL margarine, softened
250 mL very warm water,
    (49 to 54 °C)
    salad oil

Equipment:

Large mixing bowl, wooden spoon, rubber spatula, narrow metal spatula, small and large liquid and dry measures, electric mixer, large wooden board, plastic wrap, pastry brush, kitchen towel, 24 by 13 cm loaf pan, cooling rack.

Procedure:

1st Day

1. Put 250 mL flour, sugar, salt, and active dry yeast in a large bowl. Stir well with a wooden spoon.
2. Add the margarine and warm water to dry ingredients in mixing bowl.
3. Beat mixture with electric mixer (or by hand) for 2 minutes.
4. Add 125 mL more flour. Beat 1 more minute, scraping sides of bowl often.
5. Add enough of the remaining 250 mL of flour to make a soft dough. (Add the flour, a little at a time, using a wooden spoon to mix. Use just enough flour so that the dough leaves the sides of the bowl. Save the remaining flour for the next step.)
6. Turn the dough out onto a lightly floured board and knead until smooth and elastic, about 5 to 6 minutes.
7. Cover dough with plastic wrap, then a clean towel. Let rest for 15 minutes.
8. Remove plastic wrap and towel. Punch dough down by pushing your fist firmly into the center of the dough.
9. Shape dough into a loaf. (Shape dough by patting into a rectangle. Beginning with short side at the top, roll dough toward you forming a long roll. Seal ends with fingers and tuck under loaf.) Place dough in a greased 24 by 13 cm loaf pan. Brush top with oil; cover with plastic wrap. Refrigerate dough 2 to 24 hours.

2nd Day

1. Preheat oven to 200 °C.
2. Remove bread dough from refrigerator. Let stand at room temperature for 10 minutes. Puncture any gas bubbles with a greased toothpick.
3. Bake bread about 35 to 40 minutes or until done. Crust is golden brown and loaf sounds hollow when tapped with the knuckles. Turn loaf out onto rack and cool thoroughly.

Makes one 24 by 13 cm loaf.

ITALIAN BREAD

Ingredients:

525 to 675 mL flour
    7 mL sugar
    7 mL salt
    1 package active dry yeast
    7 mL margarine, softened

225 mL very warm water
    (49 to 54 °C)
cornmeal
salad oil

Equipment:

Waxed paper, small and large liquid and dry measures, narrow metal spatula, rubber spatula, wooden spoon, large mixing bowl, electric mixer, large wooden board, pastry brush, plastic wrap, kitchen towel, cookie sheet, rolling pin, sharp knife, cooling rack.

Procedure:

1st Day

1. Put flour onto a sheet of waxed paper.
2. In large mixing bowl, thoroughly mix 250 mL flour, sugar, salt and dry yeast. Add softened margarine.
3. Gradually add warm water to dry ingredients and beat 3 minutes at medium speed of electric mixer, scraping bowl occasionally.
4. Stir in enough additional flour with a wooden spoon to make a stiff dough. Use any leftover flour in the next step.
5. Turn dough out onto a lightly floured board and knead until smooth and elastic, about 5 minutes.
6. Cover dough with plastic wrap, then with a clean towel. Let rest 10 minutes.
7. Grease a cookie sheet and sprinkle with a little cornmeal.
8. Shape dough into a narrow roll about 36 cm long. (To shape dough, roll into a rectangle. Then roll jellyroll-style sealing ends with fingers.)
9. Place shaped dough on cookie sheet and brush top with oil. Cover loosely with plastic wrap. Refrigerate 2 to 24 hours.

2nd Day

1. Preheat oven to 220 °C.
2. Remove bread dough from refrigerator. Uncover carefully and let stand 10 minutes.
3. Make 3 or 4 diagonal cuts on top with a sharp knife.
4. Bake loaf about 25 minutes or until top is golden brown and loaf sounds hollow when tapped with the knuckles.
5. Put bread on cooling rack to cool thoroughly.

Makes 1 loaf.

(Note: If you like your bread brown and crusty, brush top with an egg wash about 5 minutes before bread is done. Use 1 egg white mixed with 15 mL cold water for egg wash.)

OATMEAL BREAD

Ingredients:

50	mL very warm water (49 to 54 °C)		5	mL salt
1	package active dry yeast		25	mL margarine
200	mL milk		750	mL flour
50	mL brown sugar, firmly packed		125	mL rolled oats
				salad oil

Equipment:

Custard cup, small saucepan, small and large liquid and dry measures, narrow metal spatula, rubber spatula, wooden spoon, large mixing bowl, electric mixer or rotary beater, pastry brush, plastic wrap, kitchen towel, large wooden board, 24 by 13 cm loaf pan, cooling rack.

Procedure:

1st Day

1. Put warm water into a custard cup. Sprinkle yeast over water and mix until moistened; set aside.
2. Combine milk, sugar, salt and margarine in a small saucepan. Heat until mixture feels comfortably warm on wrist (about 49 to 54 °C).
3. Put 250 mL flour in a large mixing bowl.
4. Add softened yeast and warmed milk mixture to flour. Beat with mixer (or rotary beater) until mixture is smooth, about 1 minute. Add 125 mL more flour and the rolled oats. Beat again until smooth.
5. Add enough of the remaining flour to make a soft dough. (Use the leftover flour in the next step.)
6. Turn dough out onto lightly floured board and knead until smooth and elastic (about 5 minutes).
7. Cover dough with plastic wrap and then a clean towel. Let rest 10 to 15 minutes.
8. Shape dough into a loaf. (Shape dough by patting into a rectangle. Beginning with short side at the top, roll dough toward you forming a long roll. Seal ends with fingers and tuck under loaf.) Place dough in a greased 24 by 13 cm loaf pan. Brush top with oil. Cover loosely with plastic wrap.
9. Refrigerate dough 2 to 24 hours.

2nd Day

1. Preheat oven to 200 °C.
2. Remove dough from refrigerator. Uncover and let stand 10 minutes at room temperature. Puncture any gas bubbles with a greased toothpick.
3. Bake bread for 30 to 40 minutes or until top is golden brown and loaf sounds hollow when tapped with the knuckles.
4. Turn bread out onto cooling rack to cool thoroughly.

Makes 1 loaf.

WHOLE WHEAT BREAD

Ingredients:

750	mL all-purpose flour	250	mL milk
250	mL whole wheat flour	75	mL water
25	mL sugar	30	mL margarine
10	mL salt		salad oil
1	package active dry yeast		

Equipment:

2 large mixing bowls, small and large liquid and dry measures, narrow metal spatula, rubber spatula, wooden spoon, medium saucepan, electric mixer, large wooden board, plastic wrap, kitchen towel, pastry brush, 24 by 13 cm loaf pan, cooling rack.

Procedure:

1st Day

1. Put all-purpose and whole wheat flours in a large bowl. Mix thoroughly with a wooden spoon.
2. Combine 375 mL flour mixture, sugar, salt and yeast in large mixing bowl.
3. Put milk, water and margarine into a medium saucepan. Heat over low heat until very warm (49 to 54 °C).
4. Gradually add liquid ingredients to dry ingredients and beat 2 minutes with electric mixer, scraping bowl often.
5. Add 125 mL flour mixture and beat at high speed 2 minutes.
6. Using a wooden spoon, stir in enough additional flour mixture to make a stiff dough.
7. Turn dough out onto a lightly floured board and knead until smooth and elastic, about 5 to 6 minutes.
8. Cover dough with plastic wrap, then a clean towel. Let rest 15 minutes.
9. Shape dough into a loaf. (Shape dough by patting into a rectangle. Beginning with short side at the top, roll dough toward you forming a long roll. Seal ends with fingers and tuck under loaf.) Place dough in a greased 24 by 13 cm loaf pan. Brush top with oil and cover with plastic wrap. Refrigerate 2 to 24 hours.

2nd Day

1. Preheat oven to 200 °C.
2. Remove dough from refrigerator. Let stand at room temperature for 10 minutes. Puncture any gas bubbles with a greased toothpick.
3. Bake bread about 40 minutes or until crust is brown and loaf sounds hollow when tapped with the knuckles.
4. Turn bread out onto wire cooling rack and cool thoroughly.

Makes 1 loaf.

PEASANT BREAD

Ingredients:

375 mL all-purpose flour	1 package active dry yeast
300 mL rye flour	125 mL milk
15 mL cocoa	15 mL margarine
5 mL sugar	125 mL water
5 mL salt	30 mL dark molasses
10 mL caraway seeds (optional)	salad oil

Equipment:

2 medium mixing bowls, 1 large mixing bowl, medium saucepan, small and large liquid and dry measures, narrow metal spatula, rubber spatula, wooden spoon, electric mixer, large wooden board, pastry brush, plastic wrap, kitchen towel, baking sheet, sharp knife, cooling rack.

Procedure:

1st Day

1. Put all-purpose and rye flours into separate bowls.
2. In large bowl of electric mixer, mix 250 mL of each of the flours with the cocoa, sugar, salt, caraway seeds and yeast.
3. Put milk, margarine, water and molasses into a medium saucepan. Heat until liquids are warm (about 54 °C).
4. Gradually add warm liquid ingredients to dry ingredients and beat 2 minutes on medium speed of electric mixer.
5. Add 175 mL all-purpose flour and beat on high speed 2 minutes.
6. Using a wooden spoon, gradually stir in remaining rye flour and enough all-purpose flour to make a soft dough.
7. Turn dough onto a lightly floured board and knead 8 to 10 minutes or until dough is smooth and elastic. (If dough sticks, a small amount of all-purpose flour can be added.)
8. Shape dough into a ball. Cover with plastic wrap, then a kitchen towel and let rest 20 minutes.
9. Remove plastic and punch dough down. Shape dough into a round loaf and place on a greased baking sheet.
10. Brush top of loaf with oil and cover loosely with plastic wrap. Refrigerate 2 to 24 hours.

2nd Day

1. Preheat oven to 200 °C.
2. Remove dough from refrigerator. Let stand 10 minutes. Puncture any gas bubbles with a greased toothpick.
3. With a sharp knife, cut an X in the top of loaf.
4. Bake bread 30 to 40 minutes or until loaf sounds hollow when tapped with the knuckles.
5. Cool bread on a wire cooling rack.

Makes 1 loaf.

WHEAT GERM HAMBURGER BUNS

Ingredients:

15	mL sugar	30	mL butter or margarine
15	mL salt	1	egg
1	package active dry yeast	125	mL wheat germ
600 to 750 mL all-purpose flour			salad oil
250	mL milk		

Equipment:

Large mixing bowl, medium mixing bowl, small saucepan, small and large liquid and dry measures, narrow metal spatula, rubber spatula, custard cup, electric mixer, wooden spoon, large wooden board, sharp knife, pastry brush, plastic wrap, kitchen towel, cookie sheet, cooling rack.

Procedure:

1st Day

1. Combine sugar, salt, yeast and 250 mL flour in large mixing bowl. Put remaining 500 mL flour into a separate bowl and set aside.
2. Put milk and butter or margarine into a small saucepan. Heat until very warm (54 °C).
3. Gradually add liquid ingredients to dry ingredients; blend until moistened, then beat 2 minutes with wooden spoon or electric mixer.
4. Break egg into custard cup and add to batter. Add 250 mL more flour and beat 2 more minutes.
5. Using wooden spoon, stir in wheat germ and enough additional flour to make a soft dough.
6. Turn dough onto a lightly floured board, knead 5 to 6 minutes or until dough is smooth and elastic.
7. With a sharp knife, cut dough into 8 pieces. Cover with plastic wrap, then a kitchen towel and let rest 15 to 20 minutes.
8. Grease a cookie sheet.
9. Shape each piece of dough into a ball. Flatten into rounds on cookie sheet. Brush with oil and cover with plastic wrap. Refrigerate 2 to 24 hours.

2nd Day

1. Preheat oven to 200 °C.
2. Uncover buns. Let stand 10 minutes at room temperature.
3. Bake buns 15 to 20 minutes or until golden brown.
4. Cool hamburger buns on wire cooling rack.

Makes 8 hamburger buns.

The cookie jar

CARROT COOKIES

Ingredients:

250	mL flour		100	mL sugar	
5	mL baking powder		1	egg	
1	mL salt		125	mL carrots, cooked and mashed	
125	mL shortening		125	mL shredded coconut	

Equipment:

Small liquid and dry measures, large dry measures, narrow metal spatula, fork, rubber spatula, wooden spoon, sifter, waxed paper, custard cup, large mixing bowl, electric mixer (optional), 2 small spoons, 2 cookie sheets, wide metal spatula, cooling racks.

Procedure:

1st Day

1. Put flour, baking powder and salt into sifter. Sift ingredients together onto a sheet of waxed paper.
2. Put shortening into large mixing bowl. Stir with a wooden spoon until shortening is creamy.
3. Add sugar, egg and carrots to shortening and beat well.
4. Blend in dry ingredients and coconut.
5. Cover and refrigerate dough until ready to use.

2nd Day

1. Preheat oven to 200 °C.
2. Lightly grease two cookie sheets.
3. Drop spoonfuls of dough 5 cm apart onto cookie sheets.
4. Bake cookies 8 to 10 minutes or until lightly browned.
5. Transfer cookies to cooling racks with wide spatula.

Makes 2 dozen, 5 cm cookies.

OATMEAL COOKIES

Ingredients:

250	mL flour	75	mL shortening
2	mL salt	125	mL light brown sugar, firmly packed
2	mL baking soda		
1/2	egg	50	mL granulated sugar
30	mL water	375	mL rolled oats, uncooked
3	mL vanilla		

Equipment:

Small liquid and dry measures, large dry measures, narrow metal spatula, rubber spatula, wooden spoon, electric mixer (optional), sifter, waxed paper, custard cup, fork, large mixing bowl, 2 cookie sheets, 2 small spoons, wide metal spatula, cooling racks.

Procedure:

1st Day

1. Put flour, salt and baking soda into sifter. Sift ingredients onto a sheet of waxed paper; set aside.
2. Break egg into custard cup. Beat slightly with fork and divide evenly. Share half with another group.
3. Add water and vanilla to the egg in the custard cup.
4. Put shortening, brown sugar and granulated sugar into large mixing bowl. Using wooden spoon or electric mixer, cream together until light and fluffy.
5. Add egg, water and vanilla to creamed mixture. Beat until smooth. Add sifted dry ingredients and blend well.
6. Stir in rolled oats. Cover and refrigerate dough until ready to use.

2nd Day

1. Preheat oven to 190 °C.
2. Lightly grease two cookie sheets.
3. Drop spoonfuls of dough onto cookie sheet 5 cm apart.
4. Bake cookies 10 to 12 minutes.
5. Transfer cookies to cooling racks with wide metal spatula.

Makes 2 1/2 dozen, 5 cm cookies.

Note: 50 mL chopped nuts, chocolate chips or raisins may be added to dough with rolled oats.

LEMON NUT CRISPS

Ingredients:

250	mL flour	10	mL lemon juice
3	mL baking powder	15	mL water
1	mL baking soda	50	mL margarine
1	mL salt	125	mL sugar
1/2	egg	50	mL chopped nuts
3	mL grated lemon peel		

Equipment:

Small liquid and dry measures, large dry measures, narrow metal spatula, rubber spatula, wooden spoon, sifter, waxed paper, 2 custard cups, fork, medium mixing bowl, 2 cookie sheets, 2 small spoons, wide spatula, cooling racks, cutting board, French knife, grater.

Procedure:

1st Day

1. Put flour, baking powder, baking soda and salt into sifter. Sift ingredients onto a sheet of waxed paper; set aside.
2. Break egg into custard cup. Beat with fork and divide evenly. Share half with another group.
3. Combine grated lemon peel, lemon juice and water in a custard cup.
4. Put margarine in medium mixing bowl. Stir with a wooden spoon to soften. Add sugar and beat until light and fluffy.
5. Beat in egg, lemon peel, lemon juice and water.
6. Gradually stir in dry ingredients and nuts.
7. Cover and refrigerate dough until ready to use.

2nd Day

1. Preheat oven to 190 °C.
2. Lightly grease two cookie sheets.
3. Drop spoonfuls of dough 5 cm apart onto cookie sheet.
4. Bake cookies 12 to 14 minutes or until the edges are lightly browned.
5. Transfer cookies with wide spatula to cooling racks.

Makes about 20, 5 cm cookies.

PUMPKIN COOKIES

Ingredients:

250 mL flour	125 mL margarine
2 mL baking soda	125 mL sugar
2 mL cinnamon	125 mL pumpkin, canned or cooked
1 mL salt	50 mL raisins
1/2 egg	

Equipment:

Small liquid and dry measures, large dry measures, narrow metal spatula, rubber spatula, wooden spoon, fork, sifter, small mixing bowl, medium mixing bowl, custard cup, 2 cookie sheets, 2 small spoons, wide spatula, cooling racks.

Procedure:

1st Day

1. Put flour, baking soda, cinnamon and salt into sifter. Sift ingredients together into small mixing bowl; set aside.
2. Break egg into custard cup. Stir with a fork and divide evenly. Share half with another group.
3. Put margarine into medium mixing bowl. Stir with wooden spoon until softened.
4. Add sugar to margarine. Cream until mixture is light and fluffy.
5. Add egg to creamed mixture. Blend well with wooden spoon and add pumpkin.
6. Toss raisins with dry ingredients until coated. Add to creamed mixture, mixing well.
7. Cover dough and store in refrigerator until ready to use.

2nd Day

1. Preheat oven to 190°C.
2. Lightly grease two cookie sheets.
3. Drop spoonfuls of dough about 5 cm apart onto cookie sheets.
4. Bake cookies 10 to 12 minutes or until golden brown.
5. Transfer cookies to cooling racks with wide spatula.

Makes 2 dozen, 5 cm cookies.

BROWNIES

Ingredients:

2	squares, 28 g each, unsweetened chocolate	2	mL salt	
75	mL margarine	250	mL sugar	
175	mL flour	2	eggs	
3	mL baking powder	50	mL walnuts, coarsely chopped	

Equipment:

Small liquid and dry measures, large dry measures, narrow metal spatula, rubber spatula, wooden spoon, large heavy saucepan, sifter, waxed paper, cutting board, French knife, 20 cm square baking pan, cooling rack.

Procedure:

1. Preheat oven to 180 °C.
2. Grease a 20 cm square baking pan.
3. Put chocolate and margarine into large, heavy saucepan. Melt slowly over very low heat. (Watch carefully so chocolate does not scorch.) When chocolate has melted, remove from heat and set aside.
4. Put flour, baking powder and salt into sifter. Sift ingredients onto a sheet of waxed paper; set aside.
5. Using a wooden spoon, mix sugar into melted chocolate and margarine.
6. Add eggs one at a time, beating well after each addition.
7. Add dry ingredients and walnuts, stirring until blended.
8. Spread batter evenly in pan with rubber spatula.
9. Bake brownies 25 minutes or until a toothpick inserted in the center comes out clean.
10. Transfer pan to cooling rack. Cut cooled brownies into 5 cm squares.

Makes 16 brownies.

CHOCOLATE WALNUT BARS

Ingredients:

125 mL all-purpose flour	125 mL brown sugar
125 mL whole wheat flour	30 mL molasses
50 mL whole bran cereal	1/2 egg
2 mL baking soda	50 mL chocolate chips
1 mL salt	50 mL walnuts, chopped
125 mL margarine	

Equipment:

Small liquid and dry measures, large dry measures, narrow metal spatula, rubber spatula, wooden spoon, fork, medium mixing bowl, large mixing bowl, custard cup, cutting board, French knife, 20 cm square cake pan, cooling rack.

Procedure:

1. Preheat oven to 190°C.
2. Lightly grease a 20 cm square cake pan.
3. Put both flours, bran cereal, baking soda and salt in medium mixing bowl; mix thoroughly with a wooden spoon.
4. Put margarine, brown sugar and molasses in large mixing bowl.
5. Break egg into custard cup. Mix with fork and divide evenly. Share half with another group.
6. Add egg to margarine mixture. Cream mixture with wooden spoon until light and fluffy.
7. Add dry ingredients and mix well.
8. Stir in chocolate chips and walnuts.
9. Spread mixture evenly in prepared pan.
10. Bake bars 20 minutes or until a toothpick inserted in the center comes out clean.
11. Transfer pan to cooling rack. When cookies are cool, cut into 5 cm squares.

Makes 16 cookies.

SNICKERDOODLES

Ingredients:

350 mL flour	125 mL shortening
5 mL cream of tartar	175 mL sugar
3 mL baking soda	2 mL cinnamon
1 mL salt	30 mL sugar
1 egg	

Equipment:
Small liquid and dry measures, large dry measures, narrow metal spatula, rubber spatula, wooden spoon, sifter, waxed paper, custard cup, fork, medium mixing bowl, small mixing bowl, 2 cookie sheets, wide spatula, cooling racks.

Procedure:
1st Day

1. Put flour, cream of tartar, baking soda and salt into sifter. Sift ingredients onto a sheet of waxed paper; set aside.
2. Break egg into custard cup; beat lightly with fork and set aside.
3. Put shortening into medium mixing bowl. Stir with wooden spoon to soften.
4. Add 175 mL sugar to shortening, beating until smooth. Add egg and beat mixture until smooth.
5. Stir in dry ingredients and mix well.
6. Cover and refrigerate dough until ready to use.

2nd Day

1. Preheat oven to 200 °C.
2. Lightly grease two cookie sheets.
3. Mix cinnamon and 30 mL sugar together in small mixing bowl.
4. Shape dough into 2.5 cm balls. Roll cookies in cinnamon-sugar mixture and place 5 cm apart on cookie sheets.
5. Bake cookies 8 to 10 minutes or until lightly browned.
6. Transfer cookies to cooling racks with wide spatula.

Makes 2 dozen, 5 cm cookies.

PEANUT BUTTER COOKIES

Ingredients:

125	mL margarine		3	mL vanilla
125	mL peanut butter		300	mL flour
125	mL granulated sugar		3	mL baking powder
125	mL light brown sugar, firmly packed		2	mL baking soda
1	beaten egg		2	mL salt

Equipment:

Small liquid and dry measures, large dry measures, narrow metal spatula, rubber spatula, wooden spoon, fork, large mixing bowl, custard cup, sifter, waxed paper, 2 cookie sheets, wide spatula, cooling racks.

Procedure:

1st Day

1. Put margarine, peanut butter and sugars in large mixing bowl; set aside.
2. Break egg into a custard cup. Beat with a fork and add vanilla; set aside.
3. Put flour, baking powder, baking soda and salt into sifter. Sift ingredients together onto a sheet of waxed paper; set aside.
4. Stir peanut butter mixture with wooden spoon until blended. Beat in egg and vanilla.
5. Add dry ingredients and mix well.
6. Cover dough and chill at least 1 hour.

2nd Day

1. Preheat oven to 180 °C.
2. Lightly grease two cookie sheets.
3. Shape small amounts of dough into 2.5 cm balls. Place cookies 5 cm apart on cookie sheets. Dip a fork into flour and gently flatten cookies in a crisscross pattern.
4. Bake cookies 12 to 15 minutes or until lightly browned.
5. Transfer cookies to cooling racks with wide spatula.

Makes 3 dozen, 5 cm cookies

Variation:

Follow recipe through step 2 of second day.

3. Shape cookies into 2.5 cm balls. Place 5 cm apart on a lightly greased cookie sheet. Press thumb in center of each cookie.
4. Bake cookies 10 to 12 minutes or just until set.
5. Transfer cookies to cooling racks. Fill each indentation with a spoonful of jelly.

VANILLA REFRIGERATOR COOKIES

Ingredients:

375 mL flour	5 mL vanilla
2 mL baking soda	125 mL margarine
2 mL salt	50 mL granulated sugar
1 large egg	50 mL brown sugar, firmly packed

Equipment:

Small liquid and dry measures, large dry measures, narrow metal spatula, rubber spatula, wooden spoon, sifter, waxed paper, custard cup, fork, large mixing bowl, aluminum foil, 2 cookie sheets, cutting board, sharp knife, wide spatula, cooling racks.

Procedure:

1st Day

1. Put flour, baking soda and salt into sifter. Sift ingredients together onto a sheet of waxed paper; set aside.
2. Break egg into custard cup; beat lightly with fork and add vanilla.
3. Put margarine in large mixing bowl. Stir with wooden spoon to soften.
4. Add both sugars to mixing bowl, beat until creamy. Add egg and vanilla and mix well.
5. Add dry ingredients and mix well. (Dough will be stiff.)
6. Shape dough into a long, smooth roll about 5 cm in diameter. Wrap in foil and store in refrigerator until ready to use.

2nd Day

1. Preheat oven to 200 °C.
2. Lightly grease two cookie sheets.
3. Using a sharp knife, cut chilled dough into slices 3 mm thick. Place cookies about 1.2 cm apart on baking sheet.
4. Bake cookies 6 to 8 minutes or until lightly browned.
5. Transfer cookies to cooling racks with wide spatula.

Makes 3 dozen, 5 cm cookies.

OAT CRISPIES

Ingredients:

275	mL flour	125	mL brown sugar, firmly packed
2	mL baking soda	1	egg
2	mL salt	2	mL vanilla
125	mL margarine, softened	125	mL rolled oats
125	mL granulated sugar	50	mL coconut

Equipment:

Medium mixing bowl, small liquid and dry measures, large dry measures, wooden spoon, custard cup, flour sifter, electric mixer (optional), waxed paper, aluminum foil, 2 cookie sheets, sharp knife, cutting board, wide spatula, cooling racks.

Procedure:

1st Day

1. Put flour, baking soda and salt into sifter and sift together onto a sheet of waxed paper; set aside.
2. In medium mixing bowl, beat margarine, both sugars, egg and vanilla until fluffy using a wooden spoon or electric mixer. Add sifted dry ingredients and blend well.
3. Stir in rolled oats and coconut.
4. Shape dough into a roll 5 cm in diameter and 15 cm long. Wrap well in foil and refrigerate overnight.

2nd Day

1. Preheat oven to 200 °C.
2. Lightly grease two cookie sheets.
3. Using a sharp knife, cut dough into slices, 6 mm thick. Place on cookie sheet, leaving about 5 cm between cookies.
4. Bake cookies until lightly browned, about 10 to 12 minutes.
5. Let cookies cool for 1 minute before removing from cookie sheets. Transfer cookies to cooling racks with wide spatula.

Makes 2 dozen, 5 cm cookies.

ROLLED SUGAR COOKIES

Ingredients:

625	mL flour		250	mL sugar
5	mL baking powder		2	eggs
5	mL salt		5	mL vanilla
175	mL margarine, softened			

Equipment:

Small liquid and dry measures, large dry measures, narrow metal spatula, rubber spatula, large mixing bowl, wooden spoon, sifter, waxed paper, rolling pin, wooden board or pastry cloth, cookie cutters, 2 cookie sheets, wide spatula, cooling racks.

Procedure:

1st Day

1. Sift flour, baking powder and salt onto a sheet of waxed paper; set aside.
2. Put margarine and sugar into large mixing bowl. Beat with a wooden spoon until fluffy.
3. Add eggs, one at a time, to creamed mixture, beating well after each addition. Add vanilla.
4. Stir in dry ingredients, mixing well.
5. Cover dough and chill at least 2 hours. (Dough may be stored in the refrigerator overnight.)

2nd Day

1. Preheat oven to 200 °C.
2. Lightly grease two cookie sheets.
3. Roll out dough on lightly floured board or pastry cloth to 6 mm thickness. Cut into shapes with lightly floured cookie cutters.
4. Transfer cut cookies to baking sheets with wide spatula and decorate if desired.
5. Bake cookies 6 to 8 minutes or until lightly browned.
6. Transfer cookies to cooling racks with wide spatula.

Makes 4 dozen, 5 cm cookies.

GINGERBREAD COOKIES

Ingredients:

375	mL flour	50	mL molasses
2	mL baking soda	7	mL vinegar
	pinch salt	1/2	egg
5	mL powdered ginger	50	mL margarine
1	mL cinnamon	50	mL sugar

Equipment:

Small liquid and dry measures, large dry measures, narrow metal spatula, sifter, waxed paper, small bowl, custard cup, fork, wooden spoon, large mixing bowl, electric mixer (optional), rubber spatula, aluminum foil, 2 cookie sheets, rolling pin, wooden board or pastry cloth, cookie cutters, wide spatula, cooling racks.

Procedure:

1st Day

1. Put flour, baking soda, salt, ginger and cinnamon into sifter. Sift ingredients together onto a sheet of waxed paper; set aside.
2. Combine molasses and vinegar in a small bowl; set aside.
3. Break egg into custard cup. Beat with fork and divide in half. Share with another group.
4. Put margarine and sugar into large mixing bowl. Beat until smooth with wooden spoon or electric mixer.
5. Add molasses, vinegar and egg to creamed mixture and mix well.
6. Add sifted dry ingredients to creamed mixture and mix well. (Dough will be stiff.)
7. Wrap dough in foil and refrigerate at least 3 to 4 hours.

2nd Day

1. Preheat oven to 190°C.
2. Lightly grease two cookie sheets.
3. Roll dough to a thickness of 3 mm. Cut into shapes with lightly floured cookie cutters. Transfer cut cookies to cookie sheets with wide spatula. Reroll scraps.
4. Bake cookies 8 to 10 minutes or until set.
5. Transfer cookies to cooling racks with wide spatula.

Makes 2 to 3 dozen cookies.

Variations: Gingerbread Boys and Girls

1. Prepare dough for gingerbread cookies. Roll to a thickness of 6 mm.
2. Cut gingerbread boy or girl figures from dough using cookie cutters. (You can use cardboard shapes instead of cookie cutters. Place shapes on top of dough and use a sharp knife to cut around them.)
3. Transfer cookies to greased cookie sheets. Decorate with raisins, pieces of cherries or nuts. (Or bake cookies and then decorate with icing.)
4. Bake cookies 12 to 15 minutes. Remove them carefully to a cooling rack to cool thoroughly.

Makes 7 to 8 large cookies.

8

Yummy cakes and pies

QUICK VANILLA CAKE

Ingredients:

500	mL cake flour	250	mL milk
300	mL sugar	5	mL vanilla
10	mL baking powder	1	egg
5	mL salt	50	mL shortening

Equipment:

23 cm round or square cake pan, sifter, large mixing bowl, small and large liquid and dry measures, narrow metal spatula, rubber spatula, custard cup, wooden spoon or electric mixer (optional), cooling rack.

Procedure:

1. Preheat oven to 180 °C.
2. Grease a 23 cm round or square cake pan.
3. Put flour, sugar, baking powder and salt into sifter. Sift ingredients together into a large mixing bowl.
4. Combine milk and vanilla in large liquid measure.
5. Break egg into a custard cup.
6. Add shortening and 160 mL of the milk mixture to the dry ingredients. Beat 2 minutes with an electric mixer or 300 strokes by hand.
7. Add the remainder of the milk and the egg. Beat batter 2 more minutes (or 300 strokes).
8. Pour batter into prepared pan. Bake 30 to 35 minutes or until toothpick inserted in the center comes out clean.
9. Cool 10 minutes in the pan. Then turn out onto cooling rack. Cool completely before frosting.

Makes one 23 cm cake (one layer).

BEST-EVER CHOCOLATE CAKE

Ingredients:

125 mL cocoa	125 mL margarine
250 mL boiling water	300 mL sugar
375 mL all-purpose flour	4 mL vanilla
5 mL baking soda	2 eggs
2 mL baking powder	
1 mL salt	

Equipment:

23 cm round or square cake pan, small mixing bowl, medium mixing bowl, wooden spoon, sifter, waxed paper, small and large liquid and dry measures, narrow metal spatula, rubber spatula, electric mixer, cooling rack.

Procedure:

1. Put cocoa in small mixing bowl. Add boiling water and stir; set aside to cool.
2. Preheat oven to 180 °C.
3. Grease a 23 cm round or square cake pan.
4. Put flour, baking soda, baking powder and salt into sifter. Sift ingredients together onto a sheet of waxed paper; set aside.
5. Put margarine in medium mixing bowl. Beat until creamy on medium speed of electric mixer.
6. Add sugar and vanilla to margarine and beat until fluffy.
7. Add eggs one at a time to creamed mixture, beating well after each addition.
8. Beat 5 minutes on medium speed, scraping sides of bowl often, until mixture is a light lemon color.
9. At low speed, add dry ingredients alternately with cocoa mixture beginning and ending with dry ingredients. *Do not overbeat.*
10. Pour batter into prepared pan. Bake 40 minutes or until toothpick inserted in the center comes out clean.
11. Cool in pan on cooling rack.
12. Frost with Glossy Chocolate Frosting. (See recipe on page 70.)

Makes one 23 cm cake (one layer).

CHOCOLATE-OAT-NUT CAKE

Ingredients:

175	mL all-purpose flour	50	mL margarine
2	mL salt	125	mL light brown sugar, firmly packed
3	mL baking soda	125	mL granulated sugar
10	mL unsweetened cocoa	2	eggs
125	mL rolled oats	250	mL chocolate chips
175	mL boiling water	60	mL walnuts, chopped

Equipment:

20 or 23 cm square cake pan, small and large liquid and dry measures, narrow metal spatula, rubber spatula, sifter, waxed paper, large mixing bowl, wooden spoon, cutting board, French knife, cooling rack.

Procedure:

1. Preheat oven to 180 °C.
2. Grease a 20 or 23 cm square pan.
3. Put flour, salt, baking soda and cocoa into sifter. Sift ingredients onto a sheet of waxed paper.
4. Put oats into a large mixing bowl. Add boiling water and stir; let stand 10 minutes.
5. Add margarine, both sugars and eggs to the oatmeal mixture and mix well with wooden spoon.
6. Add dry ingredients beating just until blended.
7. Fold in one-half of the chocolate chips and pour batter into prepared pan.
8. Sprinkle remaining chocolate chips and walnuts on top of batter.
9. Bake until toothpick inserted in center comes out clean, about 45 minutes.
10. Cool cake in pan. Sprinkle with powdered sugar before serving.

Makes one 20 or 23 cm cake (one layer).

CARROT PINEAPPLE CAKE

Ingredients:

175	mL all-purpose flour	75	mL oil
125	mL sugar	1	egg
3	mL baking powder	125	mL grated raw carrot
2	mL baking soda	50	mL crushed pineapple (with syrup)
2	mL cinnamon	3	mL vanilla
1	mL salt		

Equipment:

20 cm round or square cake pan, small and large liquid and dry measures, narrow metal spatula, rubber spatula, sifter, large mixing bowl, electric mixer, grater, cooling rack.

Procedure:

1. Preheat oven to 180 °C.
2. Grease a 20 cm round or square cake pan.
3. Put flour, sugar, baking powder, baking soda, cinnamon and salt into sifter. Sift ingredients into large mixing bowl.
4. Add oil, egg, carrots, pineapple (with syrup) and vanilla to dry ingredients. Beat 2 minutes on medium speed of electric mixer.
5. Pour batter into prepared pan.
6. Bake 30 to 35 minutes or until toothpick inserted in the center comes out clean.
7. Cool cake in pan. Frost with Cream Cheese Frosting. (See recipe on page 70.)

Makes one 20 cm cake (one layer).

APPLESAUCE CAKE

Ingredients:

375	mL all-purpose flour	75	mL shortening
175	mL sugar	175	mL applesauce
3	mL baking soda	1	egg
2	mL salt	3	mL vanilla
3	mL cinnamon	125	mL raisins (optional)
1	mL allspice	50	mL walnuts (optional)
1	mL cloves		

Equipment:

23 cm square cake pan, small liquid and dry measures, large dry measures, narrow metal spatula, rubber spatula, large mixing bowl, electric mixer, sifter, custard cup, cutting board, French knife, cooling rack.

Procedure:

1. Preheat oven to 180 °C.
2. Grease a 23 cm square cake pan.
3. Put flour, sugar, baking soda, salt, cinnamon, allspice and cloves into a sifter. Sift ingredients into a large mixing bowl.
4. Add shortening and applesauce to dry ingredients. Beat 2 minutes on medium speed of electric mixer.
5. Break egg into a custard cup and add vanilla. Add to dry ingredients and beat 1 minute.
6. Fold in raisins and nuts.
7. Pour batter into prepared pan. Bake 40 to 45 minutes or until toothpick inserted in center comes out clean.
8. Cool cake in pan. Before serving, sift powdered sugar over cake.

Makes one 23 cm cake (one layer).

VANILLA CREAM FROSTING

Ingredients:

30	mL margarine, softened
375	mL powdered sugar, sifted
30	mL milk
2	mL vanilla

Equipment:

Wooden spoon, small mixing bowl, sifter, small liquid and dry measures, large dry measures, narrow metal spatula.

Procedure:

1. Put softened margarine and powdered sugar in small mixing bowl. Beat until creamy with wooden spoon.
2. Add milk and vanilla, stirring until smooth. (If frosting is too thick, add more milk, a few drops at a time, until frosting reaches spreading consistency.)
3. Spread frosting on cooled cake.

Makes enough frosting to frost one 20 cm cake or 12 cupcakes.

Variations:

For orange or lemon frosting, omit vanilla and substitute appropriate juice for milk. Add 2 mL grated rind with juice.

GLOSSY CHOCOLATE FROSTING

Ingredients:

125 mL sugar
 30 mL cornstarch
  1 mL salt
  1 square, 28 g, unsweetened chocolate

125 mL boiling water
 25 mL margarine
  5 mL vanilla

Equipment:

Small and large liquid and dry measures, narrow metal spatula, wooden spoon or wire whisk, sifter, small heavy saucepan, rubber spatula.

Procedure:

1. Put sugar, cornstarch and salt into sifter. Sift ingredients together into small saucepan.
2. Break chocolate into pieces and add to dry ingredients.
3. Add boiling water to ingredients in saucepan and stir with wooden spoon or wire whisk.
4. Cook frosting over medium heat, stirring constantly, until smooth and thickened.
5. Remove frosting from heat and stir in margarine and vanilla.
6. Spread frosting on cake while frosting is hot.

Makes enough frosting to frost one 20 cm cake or 12 cupcakes.

CREAM CHEESE FROSTING

Ingredients:

300 mL powdered sugar
1/2 of an 84 g package (42 g) cream cheese
 25 mL margarine
  3 mL vanilla
     dash salt

Equipment:

Small liquid and dry measures, large dry measures, narrow metal spatula, wooden spoon, waxed paper, sifter, medium mixing bowl, rubber spatula.

Procedure:

1. Sift powdered sugar onto a sheet of waxed paper.
2. Put cream cheese and margarine in medium mixing bowl. Beat with wooden spoon until creamy.
3. Add vanilla and salt to cheese mixture, beating until smooth.
4. Gradually stir powdered sugar into cheese mixture. Continue beating with wooden spoon until frosting is smooth.
5. Spread frosting on cooled cake.

Makes enough frosting to frost one 20 cm cake or 12 cupcakes.

STANDARD PASTRY

Ingredients:

Single crust

250	mL all-purpose flour
2	mL salt
75	mL hydrogenated vegetable shortening
30	mL water

Double crust

500	mL all-purpose flour
5	mL salt
150	mL hydrogenated vegetable shortening
60	mL water

Equipment:

Large mixing bowl, small and large liquid and dry measures, narrow metal spatula, wooden spoon, fork, pastry blender or two table knives, waxed paper, rolling pin, 23 cm pie plate, cooling rack.

Procedure:

1. Put flour and salt into large mixing bowl. Mix together with wooden spoon.
2. Add shortening to flour mixture. Using a pastry blender or two knives, cut shortening into flour mixture until particles are the size of small peas.
3. Sprinkle water, 15 mL at a time, over flour-fat mixture, stirring with a fork until particles are moistened and cling together. *(Do not overmix.)*
4. Gather dough into a ball with hands. (Do not knead.)
5. Place pastry between two sheets of waxed paper. Use rolling pin to roll pastry into a circle 3 mm thick and 2.5 cm larger than the pie plate.
6. Remove top sheet of waxed paper. Carefully fold pastry into quarters and transfer to 23 cm pie plate. (Do not stretch pastry.) Trim edges so they extend 2.5 cm beyond edge of pie plate.
7. Turn under edges of pastry to form a rim. Flute edge. Prick crust with a fork.
8. Bake pie shell in a preheated 220 °C oven for 10 to 12 minutes or until lightly browned. Cool on cooling rack before filling.

Makes enough pastry for a 23 cm pie.

Note: For a double crust, divide pastry ball in half. Roll half of the pastry as instructed above and fit into pie plate. Roll second half of pastry. Pour filling into pie plate. Place top crust over filling, seal and flute edges. Make steam vents in the top crust with a sharp knife. Bake as recipe directs.

GRAHAM CRACKER CRUST

Ingredients:

75	mL butter or margarine	375	mL graham cracker crumbs
50	mL sugar		

Equipment:

Small saucepan, medium mixing bowl, large dry measures, fork, rubber spatula, 20 cm pie plate, cooling rack.

Procedure:

1. Preheat oven to 180 °C.
2. Put butter or margarine in small saucepan. Cook over low heat until melted.
3. Mix graham cracker crumbs and sugar in medium mixing bowl.
4. Add melted margarine to crumb mixture and mix thoroughly with a fork.
5. Press buttered crumbs firmly against the bottom and sides of 20 cm pie plate.
6. Bake crust 10 minutes. Transfer to cooling rack and cool completely before filling.

Makes one 20 cm crust.

APPLE PIE

Ingredients:

	pastry for a double crust, 23 cm pie	2	mL cinnamon
1	L apples, pared and sliced	15	mL margarine
125	mL sugar		

Equipment:

23 cm pie plate, waxed paper, rolling pin, paring knife, large mixing bowl, 2 forks, small and large dry measures, cooling rack.

Procedure:

1. Preheat oven to 200 °C.
2. Divide pastry into two parts. Roll one-half of pastry into a circle 3 mm thick and 2.5 cm larger than the pie plate. Line pie plate with pastry. (Do not prick crust with fork.)
3. Place apple slices in large mixing bowl. Add sugar and cinnamon and toss fruit lightly with two forks.
4. Heap apples in pastry-lined pie plate. Dot with margarine.
5. Roll remaining pastry into a circle 3 mm thick and 2.5 cm larger than the pie plate. Place crust over filling. Seal and flute edges. Cut slits in the top crust to allow steam to escape.
6. Bake pie 50 to 60 minutes or until crust is lightly browned and apples are tender. (Test apples with a fork.)
7. Transfer pie to cooling rack to cool.

Makes one 23 cm pie.

PUMPKIN PIE

Ingredients:

	20 cm unbaked pastry pie shell	1	mL ground cloves
125	mL brown sugar, firmly packed	2	eggs
5	mL cinnamon	300	mL pumpkin, canned or cooked
1	mL ginger	1	mL salt
1	mL nutmeg	300	mL milk

Equipment:

Small and large liquid and dry measures, narrow metal spatula, waxed paper, large mixing bowl, rotary beater or electric mixer, rubber spatula, cooling rack.

Procedure:

1. Preheat oven to 225 °C.
2. Prepare a 20 cm unbaked pastry pie shell. (Do not prick crust with fork.) Set aside.
3. Combine brown sugar, cinnamon, ginger, nutmeg and cloves on a sheet of waxed paper; set aside.
4. Put eggs in large mixing bowl and beat with rotary beater or electric mixer until well mixed. Add pumpkin, salt and brown sugar mixture, mix well.
5. Stir milk into pumpkin mixture and pour into prepared pie shell.
6. Bake pie at 225 °C for 15 minutes. Reduce heat to 190 °C and continue baking until a knife inserted near the center comes out clean, about 45 minutes.
7. Transfer pie to cooling rack to cool.

Makes one 20 cm pie.

LEMON CLOUD PIE

Ingredients:

Crust:

250	mL flour
2	mL salt
75	mL shortening
1	egg

Filling:

2	eggs
1	package, 85 g, lemon pudding and pie filling (not instant)
1	package, 85 g, cream cheese
50	mL sugar

Equipment:

Small and large liquid and dry measures, narrow metal spatula, 2 small mixing bowls, electric mixer, rubber spatula, wooden spoon, rolling pin, waxed paper, 23 cm pie plate, fork, small baking sheet, cooling rack, custard cup, medium saucepan, medium mixing bowl.

Procedure:

Crust:

1. Preheat oven to 200 °C.
2. Put flour, salt and shortening into a small mixing bowl. Using lowest speed of electric mixer, cut shortening into flour until pieces are the size of coarse cornmeal.
3. Add the egg and mix with a wooden spoon just until a dough forms. *(Do not overmix.)*
4. Roll pastry between two sheets of waxed paper into a thin circle about 5 cm larger than the 23 cm pie plate. Fit pastry into pie plate. Trim edges so they extend 2.5 cm beyond the edge of the pie plate. Fold edge to form rim and flute. Prick pastry with a fork in several places. Place extra pieces of pastry on a small baking sheet.
5. Bake pie shell and extra pastry pieces 12 to 15 minutes or until lightly browned.
6. Cool thoroughly on a cooling rack.

Filling:

1. Separate eggs. Place yolks in a custard cup and whites in a small mixing bowl.
2. Prepare pudding and pie filling according to package directions adding the two egg yolks. Transfer cooked pudding to a medium mixing bowl.
3. Add cream cheese to pie filling and mix well with a wooden spoon.
4. Using high speed of electric mixer, beat the two egg whites until foamy. Add sugar, 15 mL at a time, beating until stiff peaks form when beaters are raised.
5. Fold beaten egg whites into lemon mixture with rubber spatula.
6. Pour filling into baked pie shell. Chill pie at least two hours.
7. Before serving, crumble extra pieces of pastry and sprinkle the crumbs over the pie. Or the pie may be garnished with whipped cream.

Makes one 23 cm pie.

CHOCOLATE CREAM PIE

Ingredients:

	20 cm graham cracker crust pie shell, baked	2	mL salt
2	eggs	75	mL cocoa
250	mL sugar	500	mL milk
30	mL cornstarch	15	mL margarine
		5	mL vanilla

Equipment:

Small and large liquid and dry measures, narrow metal spatula, small bowl, fork, small covered container, sifter, wooden spoon (or wire whisk), medium saucepan.

Procedure:

1. Prepare a 20 cm baked graham cracker crust pie shell. Set aside.
2. Separate eggs. Place yolks in a small bowl. Beat with fork and set aside. Place whites in a covered container and refrigerate.
3. Sift sugar, cornstarch, salt and cocoa together into saucepan.
4. Add milk to dry ingredients, gradually, stirring with a wooden spoon or wire whisk until smooth.
5. Cook mixture over medium heat, stirring constantly, until it thickens and comes to a boil. Cook one minute longer.
6. Remove from heat. Add a small amount of the hot filling to the beaten egg yolks, beating well. Add the warmed eggs to the hot filling and stir until smooth. Return filling to heat and cook one more minute.
7. Remove filling from heat and add margarine and vanilla.
8. Pour filling into crust and refrigerate until well-chilled.

Makes one 20 cm pie.

FUDGE SUNDAE PIE

Ingredients:

250	mL evaporated milk	1/2	small box vanilla wafers
250	mL chocolate chips	1	L vanilla ice cream, softened
250	mL miniature marshmallows	50	mL walnuts, chopped
1	mL salt		

Equipment:

23 cm pie plate, small and large liquid and dry measures, large spoon, rubber spatula, wooden spoon, 2 L saucepan, cutting board, French knife, plastic wrap.

Procedure:

1. Put evaporated milk, chocolate chips, marshmallows and salt into heavy, 2 L saucepan. Cook over medium heat, stirring constantly with wooden spoon, until chocolate and marshmallows are melted and mixture starts to thicken. Remove chocolate sauce from heat and cool to room temperature.
2. Line bottom and sides of pie plate with vanilla wafers.
3. Spoon half of the ice cream over the wafers. Cover with half of the chocolate sauce. Repeat layers using remaining ice cream and sauce.
4. Sprinkle walnuts over top of pie. Cover with plastic wrap.
5. Freeze pie until firm, about 3 to 5 hours.

Makes one 23 cm pie.

Experimenting with special equipment

Woks are used to stir-fry foods. In the wok, oil is heated to a high temperature. Then small pieces of meat, fish, poultry and vegetables are added and tossed lightly with a wide spatula. Stir-fried foods cook quickly, so they must be watched carefully.

BEEF WITH PEPPERS

Ingredients:

500	g flank steak	1	mL pepper
30	mL soy sauce	15	mL cornstarch
1	clove garlic, minced	15	mL cold water
2	small green peppers	30	mL peanut oil
5	mL salt		

Equipment:

Wok, cutting board, French knife, medium mixing bowl, 2 custard cups, small spoon, wide spatula, small liquid and dry measures.

Procedure:

1. Cut steak into thin slices and place in medium mixing bowl.
2. Combine soy sauce and garlic in custard cup. Pour over meat strips and marinate 10 minutes.
3. Wash green peppers and slice into 6 mm strips.
4. Put salt, pepper and cornstarch in custard cup. Add cold water and stir until smooth.
5. Heat oil in wok until hot but not smoking. Add meat strips and marinade. Stir-fry 5 to 10 minutes.
6. Add green pepper strips to meat and stir-fry another 5 minutes.
7. Add cornstarch and mix well. Cook 1 minute, stirring constantly.
8. Serve beef with peppers over rice.

Serves 3 to 4.

CHICKEN CHOP SUEY

Ingredients:

1	whole chicken breast	5	mL sugar
45	mL soy sauce	1	mL salt
50	mL mushrooms (optional)	30	mL water
1	large carrot	125	mL bean sprouts
1	large stalk celery	15	mL cornstarch (mixed with
1/2	small onion		30 mL water)
45	mL peanut oil		

Equipment:

Wok, cutting board, French knife, small mixing bowl, custard cup, wide spatula, small and large liquid and dry measures.

Procedure:

1. Place chicken breast on cutting board. Cut into 1 cm pieces. Put chicken pieces in small mixing bowl.
2. Add 15 mL soy sauce to chicken and marinate 10 minutes.
3. Clean mushrooms, carrot, celery and onion. Cut into diagonal pieces about 3 mm thick. Set aside.
4. Heat 15 mL oil in wok until hot but not smoking. Add chicken and marinade. Stir-fry just until chicken is tender, 3 to 5 minutes. Empty contents of wok into mixing bowl and set aside.
5. Add remaining oil (30 mL) to wok. Add vegetables and quickly coat with oil. Stir-fry 2 more minutes.
6. Add remaining soy sauce (30 mL), sugar, salt and 30 mL water to vegetables. Cook several more minutes or until vegetables are crisp-tender.
7. Add bean sprouts and chicken to wok. Stir to combine with vegetables.
8. Mix cornstarch and water in a custard cup. Add to chicken and vegetables. Cook and stir until sauce thickens. Cook 1 minute longer.
9. Serve chop suey over rice.

Serves 3 to 4.

Some fondue pots are heated with alcohol burners or canned heat. Electric fondue pots have thermostats to regulate heat. Dessert fondues require low temperatures. Cheese fondues require medium temperatures. Oil fondues for cooking meat require high temperatures.

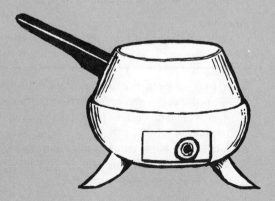

PIZZA FONDUE

Ingredients:

1 envelope onion soup mix	375 mL cheddar cheese, grated
1 can, 425 g, tomato sauce	1 loaf French bread, cut
15 mL Worcestershire sauce	into 2.5 cm cubes
5 mL oregano	

Equipment:

Electric fondue pot, fondue forks, small liquid and dry measures, large dry measures, grater, waxed paper, wooden spoon, cutting board, bread knife.

Procedure:

1. Combine onion soup mix, tomato sauce, Worcestershire sauce and oregano in fondue pot. Heat on medium setting until sauce is warm.
2. Add cheese to sauce, a little at a time, stirring constantly until cheese melts.

To Eat:

Each guest spears a cube of bread on a fondue fork. The bread is dipped into the fondue, then transferred to a regular fork. Guests take turns dipping bread into the fondue.

Serves 12 to 16.

CHOCOLATE FONDUE

Ingredients:

2 squares, 28 g each, unsweetened chocolate	45 mL margarine
125 mL sugar	dash salt
75 mL milk	4 drops orange or lemon extract

Equipment:

Electric fondue pot, fondue forks, wooden spoon, large liquid and dry measures.

Procedure:

1. Put chocolate in fondue pot and melt at very low setting.
2. Add sugar, milk, margarine and salt to chocolate. Mix well with a wooden spoon.
3. Cook sauce at medium setting, stirring constantly, until thickened. Then turn temperature setting to low. Add orange or lemon extract.
4. Using fondue forks, spear pieces of fruit, cake or marshmallows and dip into sauce.

Suggested fondue dippers: Strawberries, banana chunks, apple slices, seedless grapes, pineapple chunks, angel food or pound cake cut into bite-sized pieces, marshmallows.

A double boiler is a saucepan which fits closely into another saucepan. The lower pan holds a small amount of boiling or simmering water. The steam created by the hot water gently heats the food in the upper pan.

MACARONI AND CHEESE

Ingredients:

250	mL macaroni		30	mL margarine
30	mL flour		250	mL milk
2	mL salt		250	mL cheddar cheese, shredded
	dash pepper			

Equipment:

Double boiler, medium saucepan, colander, custard cup, wooden spoon or wire whisk, 1 L casserole dish, small and large liquid and dry measures, rubber spatula.

Procedure:

1st Day

1. Cook macaroni in lightly salted water according to package directions. Drain in colander and set aside.
2. Combine flour, salt and pepper in custard cup.
3. Put 3 cm water in the bottom of double boiler; bring to a simmer.
4. Put margarine in the top of the double boiler and place over the simmering water. Heat until melted.
5. Using a wooden spoon or wire whisk, blend flour and seasonings with melted margarine until smooth.
6. Add cold milk slowly, stirring constantly, until mixture is smooth. Cook white sauce over simmering water, stirring constantly, until thickened. Cook 1 minute longer.
7. Remove sauce from heat and add cheese. Stir sauce gently with wooden spoon until cheese melts.
8. Add cooked macaroni to cheese sauce and stir to blend. Pour into greased casserole dish. Cover and refrigerate until ready to bake.

2nd Day

1. Preheat oven to 180 °C.
2. Bake macaroni and cheese 15 to 20 minutes or until bubbly.

Serves 3 to 4.

CUSTARD SAUCE

Ingredients:

500 mL milk, scalded	1 mL salt
3 egg yolks	2 mL vanilla
50 mL sugar	

Equipment:

Double boiler, medium saucepan, small and large liquid and dry measures, 2 custard cups (for separating eggs), wire whisk, large metal spoon, rubber spatula, covered container.

Procedure:

1. Put milk in medium saucepan. To scald milk, heat the milk at a low temperature until it steams. A few bubbles may appear around the edges of the pan when the milk is ready. *(Do not let the milk boil.)*
2. While milk is heating, put water in the bottom section of the double boiler to a depth of 3 cm. Bring to a simmer.
3. Meanwhile, separate eggs. Place egg yolks in top section of double boiler. Beat with wire whisk until blended.
4. Add sugar and salt to egg yolks, beating until smooth.
5. Add scalded milk gradually to yolk mixture, beating constantly with whisk.
6. Insert top of double boiler into bottom section. Cook custard sauce over barely simmering water, stirring constantly with wire whisk, until custard will coat the back of a metal spoon. This will take about 20 minutes. *(Be sure water does not boil.)*
7. Remove custard from heat immediately and set the top of the double boiler in ice water to cool. Stir gently until custard has cooled. Add vanilla and pour into a covered container. Chill well.
8. Serve custard sauce over cobblers, steamed puddings or fruit.

Makes 250 mL sauce.

WONDER FUDGE

Ingredients:

375 mL powdered sugar	50 mL corn syrup
50 mL margarine	5 mL vanilla
250 mL chocolate chips	500 mL Rice Krispies cereal

Equipment:

Double boiler, 20 cm square cake pan, sifter, waxed paper, rubber spatula, wooden spoon, small liquid and dry measures, large dry measures.

Procedure:

1. Butter a 20 cm square cake pan.
2. Sift powdered sugar onto a sheet of waxed paper.
3. Put 3 cm water in the bottom of double boiler and bring to a simmer.
4. Combine margarine, chocolate chips, corn syrup and vanilla in top of double boiler. Cook over barely simmering water, stirring constantly with a wooden spoon until smooth. Remove from heat.
5. Add powdered sugar, stirring to blend.
6. Add cereal. Using rubber spatula, mix together until cereal is evenly coated.
7. Press mixture evenly into prepared pan.
8. Refrigerate until firm. Cut into squares.

Makes 16 pieces of candy.

Three basic pieces of equipment are needed to deep-fat fry foods: a deep pan, a wire basket to hold the food, and a skimmer to turn food in the fat and remove food from the fat. A frying thermometer should be used with nonelectric fryers to be sure the fat is kept at the right temperature.

When frying, the fat should cover the food completely. Do not try to fry too much food at one time. Do not use olive oil, butter or margarine.

After frying, strain fat through a very fine sieve or a piece of cheesecloth. Store fat in an airtight container in the refrigerator.

CHICKEN NUGGETS

Ingredients:

3	whole chicken breasts, skinned and boned	3	mL salt
1	egg, slightly beaten	10	mL sesame seeds
125	mL water	125	mL flour
			oil for frying

Equipment:

Deep-fat fryer, cutting board, French knife, pie plate, cooling rack, skimmer, paper towels, waxed paper, jelly roll pan, small and large liquid and dry measures, rubber spatula, small mixing bowl, small saucepan, wooden spoon, wire whisk.

Procedure:

1. Cut chicken breasts into 3 cm pieces.
2. Combine egg, water, salt, sesame seeds and flour in pie plate. Stir with wire whisk.
3. Dip chicken pieces in batter. Drain coated pieces on cooling rack placed over a sheet of waxed paper.
4. Put oil in deep-fat fryer, filling no more than one-third full. Heat oil to 190 °C. Line jelly roll pan with paper towels.
5. Carefully add chicken pieces, a few at a time, to hot oil. Fry 3 to 5 minutes or until golden brown. Transfer cooked pieces to paper towels in jelly roll pan with skimmer.
6. Keep chicken pieces warm in low oven while frying the rest. Serve with dill sauce or royal sauce.

Serves 6.

Dill Sauce:

50	mL sour cream	2	mL dill weed
50	mL mayonnaise	15	mL chopped dill pickle

Put all ingredients in small mixing bowl. Mix well with wooden spoon. Chill in covered container.

Royal Sauce:

125	mL catsup	15	mL vinegar
1	mL dry mustard	30	mL oil
7	mL brown sugar		

Put all ingredients in small saucepan. Mix well with wooden spoon. Heat over low heat until bubbly.

CINNAMON PUFFS

Ingredients:

oil for frying
50 mL sugar

1 mL cinnamon
1 package, 112 g, refrigerated biscuits

Equipment:

Deep-fat fryer, cutting board, French knife, small liquid and dry measures, large dry measure, small mixing bowl, skimmer, jelly roll pan, paper towels.

Procedure:

1. Heat oil in deep-fat fryer until hot but not smoking. (Use temperature setting recommended for drop doughnuts, usually 190 °C.)
2. Mix sugar and cinnamon in small mixing bowl. Line jelly roll pan with paper towels.
3. Cut each biscuit into quarters.
4. Carefully put biscuits into hot oil in a single layer. Fry 1 to 2 minutes on each side until golden brown.
5. With skimmer, transfer puffs to paper towels in jelly roll pan.
6. Roll puffs in cinnamon-sugar mixture.

Makes 40 puffs.

HOMEMADE POTATO CHIPS

Ingredients:

3 medium baking potatoes
oil for frying
salt

Equipment:

Deep-fat fryer, floating edge vegetable peeler, cutting board, French knife or slicer-grater or food processor, skimmer, paper towels, jelly roll pan.

Procedure:

1. Scrub and pare potatoes. Cut into very thin slices using knife, slicer-grater or food processor.
2. Rinse potato slices well under cold water and pat dry with paper towels.
3. Put oil in deep-fat fryer and heat to 190 °C. Line jelly roll pan with paper towels.
4. Fry potatoes, a few at a time, until golden brown, about 3 to 5 minutes. (Stir potatoes occasionally to keep them from sticking.)
5. Drain potato chips on paper towels in jelly roll pan. Season with salt.

Makes about 1 L chips.

Note: Preparation can be a 2-day process. Complete steps 1 and 2 the first day. Cover potato slices with water and refrigerate. (You will have to sacrifice some vitamins for time.) The next day, dry the potato slices well to prevent oil spatters. Complete steps 3, 4 and 5.

A crêpe pan should have a smooth surface so the crêpes will not stick. It should have shallow sloping sides so the crêpes can be flipped easily. Crêpe pans can be used to make both omelets and crêpes. Most crêpe pans require special seasoning and care. Follow the manufacturer's directions.

BASIC CRÊPE RECIPE

Ingredients:

3	eggs		1	mL salt
150	mL milk		45	mL peanut oil
150	mL water		250	mL instantized flour

Equipment:

Crêpe pan, large mixing bowl, rotary beater or electric mixer, rubber spatula, pastry brush, small and large liquid and dry measures, wide spatula, waxed paper, dinner plate.

Procedure:

1. Beat eggs in large mixing bowl with rotary beater or electric mixer until well blended.
2. Add milk, water, salt and oil to eggs; mix well.
3. Gradually add flour, beating batter until smooth.
4. Let batter stand 30 minutes in the refrigerator.
5. Place crêpe pan over moderately high heat and brush lightly with oil. Test pan with a few drops of water. (Water should sizzle.)
6. Pour a scant 50 mL of batter into the pan. Quickly tilt pan to evenly coat bottom.
7. When bubbles appear, lift one edge of the crêpe. If the underside is lightly browned, turn crêpe with a flexible spatula and cook another 15 to 20 seconds. (This side will not brown well.)
8. Stack crêpes on plate, separated by squares of waxed paper, until ready to use.

Makes about 20 crêpes.

Note: Crêpe batter should be thin, about the consistency of heavy cream. Thin batter with water, a few drops at a time, if necessary.

If you are planning to refrigerate or freeze the crêpes for later use, place squares of waxed paper between crêpes. Then wrap in aluminum foil.

Crêpes can be stored up to 2 days in the refrigerator and up to 4 months in the freezer.

CHICKEN MUSHROOM CRÊPES

Ingredients:

30 mL margarine	5 mL onion, minced
30 mL flour	2 mL salt
250 mL milk	dash pepper
175 mL cooked chicken, cut into small pieces	6 crêpes
50 mL mushrooms, canned and sliced	30 mL grated Parmesan cheese

Equipment:

Small saucepan, wooden spoon or wire whisk, medium mixing bowl, 1 L baking dish, small and large liquid and dry measures, rubber spatula, cutting board, French knife.

Procedure:

1. Preheat oven to 180 °C.
2. Melt margarine in small saucepan. Add flour, all at once, and stir with wooden spoon or wire whisk until smooth. Add milk, gradually, stirring until smooth.
3. Cook sauce over moderate heat until thickened, stirring constantly.
4. Pour half of white sauce into mixing bowl. Add chicken, mushrooms, onion, salt and pepper, mixing well with rubber spatula.
5. Spoon 30 mL creamed chicken in the center of each crêpe. Roll crêpes and transfer to baking dish.
6. Pour remaining sauce over filled crêpes and sprinkle with cheese.
7. Bake crêpes at 180 °C for 15 to 20 minutes.

Makes 6 crêpes.

STRAWBERRY SUNDAE CRÊPES

Ingredients:

500 mL fresh strawberries	6 crêpes, warmed
125 mL powdered sugar	vanilla ice cream
2 mL rum extract	

Equipment:

Paring knife, medium mixing bowl, spoon, small and large liquid and dry measures.

Procedure:

1. Wash and hull strawberries. Slice strawberries in half and put in medium mixing bowl.
2. Add powdered sugar and rum extract to strawberries and let berries stand up to 1 hour.
3. Spoon 30 mL fruit into each warmed crêpe and roll. Keep warm in low oven until ready to serve.
4. Serve crêpes on individual dessert plates topped with vanilla ice cream.

Makes 6 filled crêpes.

Note: If fresh strawberries are not available, substitute 500 mL frozen sliced strawberries and omit extra sugar.

FRENCH OMELET

Ingredients:

3	eggs		dash pepper
45	mL milk	15	mL margarine
	dash salt		

Equipment:

Crêpe pan, small mixing bowl, wire whisk or rotary beater, small liquid and dry measures, wide spatula.

Procedure:

1. Put eggs in small bowl. Using a wire whisk or rotary beater, beat eggs until they are fluffy.
2. Add milk and seasonings to eggs and mix well.
3. Put margarine in crêpe pan and melt over low heat.
4. Pour egg mixture into hot pan. Cook slowly, keeping heat low. As bottom of omelet sets, lift cooked edges with spatula and let uncooked portion flow underneath.
5. As soon as omelet has set, fold in half and serve immediately.

Serves 3 to 4.

For variety: Fill omelet with 25 mL of one of the following before folding: crisp bacon bits, minced ham, thinly sliced cooked mushrooms, sautéed tomatoes.

Just for fun

WACKY CAKE

Ingredients:

375	mL flour	5	mL vinegar
2	mL salt	5	mL vanilla
45	mL cocoa	75	mL salad oil
5	mL baking soda	250	mL water
250	mL sugar		

Equipment:

Sifter, 20 cm square cake pan, small and large liquid and dry measures, wooden spoon, cooling rack.

Procedure:

1. Preheat oven to 180 °C.
2. Put flour, salt, cocoa, baking soda and sugar into a sifter. Sift ingredients into a 20 cm square cake pan.
3. Make 3 holes in dry ingredients. Put vinegar in the first hole; vanilla in the second hole; and salad oil in the third hole.
4. Pour water over cake ingredients. Mix very well with wooden spoon.
5. Bake 25 to 30 minutes. Cool on cooling rack. Frost, if desired.

Makes one 20 cm cake.

TWO INGREDIENT MUFFINS

Ingredients:
500 mL vanilla ice cream
500 mL self-rising flour

Equipment:
Muffin pan, medium mixing bowl, wooden spoon, large dry measures, 2 small spoons.

Procedure:
1. Preheat oven to 210 °C.
2. Grease a 12 cup muffin pan well.
3. Put ice cream into a mixing bowl. Stir with a wooden spoon to soften.
4. Add flour to ice cream and beat until smooth.
5. Using 2 spoons, fill muffin cups about 3/4 full.
6. Bake muffins until golden brown, about 20 to 25 minutes. Serve warm.

Makes 12 muffins.

PUDDING-WICHES

Ingredients:
125 mL peanut butter, creamy
375 mL cold milk
1 package, 85 g, instant pudding (vanilla flavor)
24 graham crackers or chocolate wafers

Equipment:
Small deep mixing bowl, electric mixer or rotary beater, rubber spatula, large liquid and dry measures.

Procedure:
1. Put peanut butter in a small deep mixing bowl. Add milk gradually, blending with rubber spatula until smooth.
2. Add pudding mix to peanut butter mixture. Beat slowly with rotary beater or at lowest speed of electric mixer until well blended (about 2 minutes).
3. Let pudding stand 5 minutes.
4. Spread filling on 12 of the crackers. Top with remaining crackers.
5. Wrap each pudding-wich in plastic wrap.
6. Freeze sandwiches until firm, about 3 hours.

Makes 12 sandwiches.

IMPOSSIBLE PIE

Ingredients:

125 mL all-purpose baking mix	45 mL margarine
125 mL sugar	5 mL vanilla
4 eggs	1 package, 116 g, coconut
500 mL milk	

Equipment:

Blender, 23 cm pie plate, small and large liquid and dry measures, custard cup, rubber spatula, cooling rack.

Procedure:

1. Preheat oven to 200 °C.
2. Butter a 23 cm pie plate.
3. Put baking mix and sugar in blender container.
4. Break eggs, one at a time, into a custard cup; add to blender container.
5. Put milk, margarine, vanilla and coconut into blender container.
6. Blend all ingredients on medium speed until well mixed.
7. Pour filling into pie plate.
8. Bake pie 30 minutes or until lightly browned. (Knife inserted near the center should come out clean.)
9. Cool on cooling rack. Refrigerate until well chilled.

Makes one 23 cm pie.

Photo credits

Photographs used in this book were obtained from the following sources: cover, General Mills, Inc.; page 4, Coppes Kitchens; page 8, Carnation Co.; page 13, California Tree Fruit Agreement; page 20, Green Giant; page 28, Swift and Co.; page 41, Self-Rising Flour and Corn Meal Program; page 54, Fisher Nut Co., Div. of Beatrice Foods Co.; page 66, Richardson Candy Co., Div. of Beatrice Foods Co.; page 75, Hamilton Beach, Div. of Scovill; page 85, Self-Rising Flour and Corn Meal Program.

Index

Recipes are listed by categories in the Contents on pages 2 and 3.

ISBN 0—87006—293—X

BINDING SLIP
– FOR –
ESIS, ETC. WHICH <u>DO NOT</u>

ING PATTERN FOR BOOKS,
LS, ETC. WHICH REQUIRE

AN BINDERY, INC.
HESTER, INDIANA 46962

RY USE ONLY			▼
MAT.	GUM FILL.	LAMINATE	
		OVER 12"	UNDER 12"
ASE	SPECIAL		FLAT
SIVE	SINGER	NATIONAL	SADDLE
BK.	BK. PAM	MUSIC BK. PAM	PAM
	RUB SENT	NEW	MISC.

COVER SIZE	PANEL LINES	JOB NO. 277
X		COVER NO. 185